What the Church Might Learn from Jazz

What the Church Might Learn from Jazz

Drawn into the Swing of Sanctifying Significance

Brian Fraser

RESOURCE *Publications* · Eugene, Oregon

WHAT THE CHURCH MIGHT LEARN FROM JAZZ
Drawn into the Swing of Sanctifying Significance

Resource Publications
An Imprint of Wipf and Stock Publishers
199 W. 8th Ave., Suite 3
Eugene, OR 97401

www.wipfandstock.com

PAPERBACK ISBN: 979-8-3852-7002-6
HARDCOVER ISBN: 979-8-3852-7003-3
EBOOK ISBN: 979-8-3852-7004-0

VERSION NUMBER 05/21/26

For the ecclesiastical creatives
who are improvising with the great affirmations of the gospel
to reformulate the church's missioning

Contents

Introduction

The tried-and-true ways of being church are unraveling. That is true not only in North America, but in all those places to which we have exported our ways of being church. The imperial model of church promoted by Western and Eastern Europeans and their colonized acolytes around the world for so many generations is not, and never was, a faithful way of being ambassadors of God's forgiveness and reconciliation in Jesus of Nazareth, the Creator's Christ, made known by their Spirit.

The strands that have unraveled, however, are still strong. Whatever reformulations of the church emerge from this crisis will be rewoven with the strands of welcoming, worshiping, learning, and service. Is there, then, an organization that models at least some of the dynamics that will nourish this reweaving of the church to flourish anew?

I think so.

It's a jazz band playing in a dance hall in a seedy part of town where pain and suffering dominate, but hope and healing germinate. The people drawn into that space of grace, no matter how flawed and feeble they have been, sense the promise of a sanctifying significance that has been sown deep in their souls. They know that the musicking cultivates that mercy and grace. There is hope and healing in the hospitality. It's not perfect, but it's better than the callous meanness of their streets and workplaces. Maybe, just maybe, the musicking will provoke growth in that hope and healing so they can be more resonant and resilient ambassadors of the sanctifying significance they have felt there.[1]

This book suggests that the church would benefit greatly from unlearning many of its old ways of formulating its witnessing and relearning to compose itself in new ways in its new contexts. I am convinced that the wit, wisdom, and workings of the jazz community contain several seminal insights that will provoke us to imagine and implement new patterns of missioning in companionship with and faithfulness to God. I hope you are intrigued enough to play along a bit further and risk being drawn into a new swing of sanctifying significance for your church.

Whence this book

In 2002, I lost a position in the church that I loved. I was disciplined for conduct unbecoming of a minister of the gospel and suspended for two years from the ministry of Word and Sacraments of The Presbyterian Church in Canada. That meant I lost my job as dean of St. Andrew's Hall and professor of history at Vancouver School of Theology.

The subsequent years were a time of humiliating pain and resilient recovery. For me, the church was a space where that recovery was nurtured. In the hospitality of forgiving and reconciling love being offered, the cycle of traumatization and self-sabotage was broken. New attitudes and behaviors were cultivated. A transformed life is emerging and continues to be composed.

I retrained as a coach and a consultant in organizational flourishing and the leadership best suited to generate, sustain and enhance it. I started by own company called Jazzthink. I designated myself Lead Provocateur, a title that garnered a lot of attention and positive comments. That title came from a passage in the Letter to the Hebrews in the New Testament, drawn to my attention by a dear friend and mentor amid the transitions going on in my life.

1. My intrigue with using the dance hall image was sparked by finding Cressey's study of the social dynamics of the dance halls of Chicago. Cressey, *The Taxi-Dance Hall.*

> Let us hold fast to the confession of our hope without wavering, for he who has promised is faithful. And let us consider how to provoke one another to love and good deeds, not neglecting to meet together, as is the habit of some, but encouraging one another.[2]

We read it in the New Revised Standard Version translation. The Greek word *paroxumos* used in Hebrews has a number of connotations—stimulate, stir up, spur on, irritate, and provoke. The translators of the NRSV used "provoke." I like the feel and flow of that translation.

The dynamic of provoking, literally "calling forth," as I understand it, is not one of negative aggression, as is one common usage in our culture. For me, a provocative contribution involves sensing and articulating the Spirit's life-generating influence in a situation, how the Spirit is stirring up new possibilities for improvements, and aligning with the Spirit to call forth more of the forgiving and reconciling love that will improve things.

My purpose with Jazzthink was to call forth the positive potential of organizations and their leadership. My approach is to convene provocative conversations that generate flourishing communities. Most of my work is with nonprofits, many of which were faith-based. Over the past 15 years, I have been working half-time with one of the organizations with whom I consulted, Brentwood Presbyterian Church in Burnaby, BC. This book owes much to them.

My hook, or unique value proposition, in Jazzthink was offering jazz as a model for innovation and resilience in a community's attitudes and behaviors throughout their networks of benefit. I encourage and equip them to do so through the most common form of jazz in human experience, ordinary conversation.

By the age of 13, most humans have put in the recommended 10,000 hours of practice to be adept in the art of conversation. We have become sufficiently competent in vocabulary and grammar to engage in complex conversations about the things that matter most to us. We can contribute constructively to those conversations to

2. Hebrews 10:23–25a (NRSV).

make our networks better spaces in which to flourish. We can be the blessings we are designed to be. We can discover our sanctifying significance for the common good of the world.

We can, but we often don't.

Exploring the dynamics of that traumatic tragedy of "can but don't" will be seminal in these devotional dialogues. Why do we inflict violent subversion on our God-given potential for sanctifying significance in the midst of a culture addicted to shaming and shunning? What would be different if we awakened to our true capacity for co-creating with God and each other a flourishing future one conversation after another? What can jazz teach us about doing that?

I am not a jazz musician. My place in the complex dynamic of jazz musicking is in the audience, being inspired and informed by the mysteries and meanings that get conveyed in the music. I am, in the root sense of the word, an "amateur," one who loves and seeks to understand more fully.

What I bring to this loving/learning process is 79 years of Christian praxis within the networks and traditions of The Presbyterian Church in Canada. This book is a progress report on how that matrix of inspirations and influences continues to be composed in conversation with those dimensions of the jazz community I have encountered thus far.

Whence this format?

This book took shape in the mysterious discipline of personal prayer. It is not a discipline I practiced much until the COVID pandemic struck my networks in March of 2020. Then it became, thanks to the invitation of a Buddhist friend, a daily early morning activity, with a few lapses into laziness.

Different people pray in different ways. As my practice developed, it became a dialogue with God, with others who had been drawn into our conversations, and with the significant self God was nourishing to flourish within and through me. This was a learning space for wondering what would happen if we considered it this way, if we explored these possibilities, if we put this combination of words together, if we tried this way of playing/praying.

I was praying and playing jazz with the church's house trio—the Holy Trinity, Creator, Ambassador, and Reformer. I improvised with a variety of names for the God with whom I was in daily conversation. "Friend" was important in the early stages of establishing the discipline. Randy Woodley's *Indigenous Theology and the Western Worldview*, suggests the term "Community of Creator."[3] My improvisation on that phrase is "Family of Creator." It ties the intimacy of dancing in friendship with the community of the divine Family to my longing to belong, to be accepted and appreciated, to become increasingly aware of my deep sanctifying significance in the interdependencies of the family of creation.

In whatever ways we seek to name how the Divine Energy is revealed to us as forgiving and reconciling love for the whole world, they are a family of self-giving love that is dancing around (*perichoresis*) in delight at all the possibilities that are being generated as God's flourishing future meets our traumatized present. That dynamic—a redeeming future meeting a ruptured present—is the life-flow of jazz.

This book, then, is a progress report in prayer on the reformulation of my understanding of my Christian faith as the Family of Creator has illumined my ponderings and participation in the family business of caring for creation over the past five years and a bit.

Whence this faith

I was born and bred, and remain, a Canadian Presbyterian. That's the network of pondering the Christian faith from which I live and move and have my being, with all of its benefits and risks. These conversations have awakened me to both. They have made me more deeply aware of the dynamics of being treasures in earthen

3. Woodley, *Indigenous Theology and the Western Worldview*, 49.

vessels and seeing through a glass darkly, as Paul cautioned the Corinthians.

This Canadian network of John Calvin's heirs has had a particular fascination with Paul's letters to the Corinthian church(es). They were caught up in the stormy forming of their communal consciousness as Christians among that first generation of ambassadors (*presbeuos*) of the sanctifying significance that the Family of Creator was cultivating in and through them. They were composing a constructive consciousness of what it meant to live in and out of the melodies, rhythms and harmonies of God's love as revealed most clearly in Jesus, the Christ, and made real for us in the sanctifying workings of the Holy Spirit.

According the traditions of Canadian Presbyterians, the great affirmation of the gospel is that God was in Christ forgiving and reconciling the world and made us ambassadors of that message (2 Corinthians 5:19–21). That is the core truth of the gospel from which we are summoned to innovate in the context of the sufferings of the people among whom God has placed us to spread blessing.

Learning more about how that reality is unfolding in our time remains the focus of my conversations in the life of Brentwood Presbyterian Church, with whom I am currently missioning. The substance of the conversations comes from the broad range of voices that show up in my library, in the insights that arise from my engagement with social media, in the conversations through which we co-create the church and its missioning, and in the early morning prayers that bring all of this information and knowledge into an inspiring wisdom for the day. I have been drawn further into the reality of God's kinship and commonweal through these conversations that originated in the disruptions of the COVID pandemic and have continued to this day.

Whence this approach

For almost a century now, Karl Barth has provoked the ponderings of Canadian Presbyterians. His insights on doing theology in prayer have taken deep root in me, especially in this latest stage of my disciplines of praying.[4] My praying, in the form you will encounter in this book, shapes my attitudes and behaviors in Christ's missioning.

The free verse style of writing these prayers came to my attention early in my life when I found the sermons and prayers of Peter Marshall on my parents' bookshelves. Marshall was a Presbyterian minister in the United States and, for a time, chaplain to the US Senate. His style of writing gradually became for me a favored way of composing my sermons and prayers.

When I was ordained to the office of Minister of Word and Sacraments in The Presbyterian Church in Canada in 1978, I agreed that "the standards" of Christ's church were being entrusted with "a special degree of responsibility for their care" to me as a contributor to this office in the church's government and I vowed, "in obedience to Scripture and under the promised guidance of the Holy Spirit," to contribute to "the church's continuing function of reformulating the faith." I have always seen this as a collegial responsibility, in keeping with the best interpretations of the Presbyterian tradition. A key standard of our tradition is that we are to "take away all occasion for tyranny" by ensuring full participation in the decisions that reformulate the church's missioning in order to enable full responsibility in carrying that missioning out. If we are to care for the manifest church as the Holy Spirit guides us, I think we need to resist the strong tendency today to give authority over to autocratic individuals or cliques who claim to know what is best for the church. I also think we need to resist the strong temptation today to see the church as a righteous haven in a heartless world that has a monopoly on the truth. You will find those biases throughout these devotions.

My fascination with jazz began on my first day in Toronto in 1965 when I took up residence at Knox College and began my studies in history at the University of Toronto. The tradition at Knox was to settle into your dorm room briefly, then head downtown to Sam the Record Man's. As I was exploring the store in

4. Barth, *Prayer*.

wonderment, I encountered a display of Oscar Peterson's *Canadiana Suite* on sale for $3.99. That musicking brought intuition and emotion to my intellectual approach to Canadian history and, within that field, a particular fascination with the organizational and leadership history of Canadian Presbyterianism. The path from there to this book has seen many twists and turns, but there is a clear trajectory towards sensing jazz as a model for a flourishing church.

Another dynamic I've come to realize is that the Spirit is actively working in and through the jazz community. Church scholars often talk about the 'visible" church and the "invisible" church, or the "manifest" church and the "latent" church. For me, these ideas refer primarily to the church as we encounter it as a community in and, ideally, for the world. That's the "visible" church. The "invisible" church refers to those communities in which the Spirit is actively generating forgiving and reconciling love without that work needing to be explicitly labeled as "Christian." In my experience, especially in conversations, folks in the jazz community are very much part of that "invisible" church.

The image of churches as "dance halls" came recently on this journey of reformulation. Such places have a seedy and sordid history. But in the midst of those earthen vessels, people found belonging, connection, and significance. It was fleeting and hardly satisfying in most cases. But it did happen in a world and among people who were increasingly being demeaned, marginalized, and oppressed. If all of the human distortions and delusions were transformed by a divine owner who acted like Jesus of Nazareth with the people he hung out with in the Galilee of his day (remember the Samaritan woman in John 4:1–30), what blessing might such places be in our shaming and traumatizing world? Can we imagine the manifest church as the Family of Creator's dance halls where we connect and dance in delight to the swing of the musicking of the Trinity Trio and whoever the rest of the band is for that gathering? While very different in the quality of connecting and relating that the church offers at its best, the longing for acceptance and significance that filled those dance halls remains the same. I hope these prayers awaken your appreciation for your sanctifying significance in being satisfied and in satisfying.

The flow of these ponderings is a bit like a jazz suite. It moves along this trajectory. We begin with a Prelude that explores the lessons that we, as church, might discover in our encounter with the art of jazz. In the first movement we will consider God's call, the initiative the Spirit of the Creator's Christ is taking to nourish us in our sanctifying significance in flourishing in the family business of caring for creation. In the second movement, we will consider humanity's response to that call in its striving for freedom. In the third movement, we will consider what it means to learn to dance more freely and fruitfully within and through institutions, such as the church and the jazz community. In a postlude, we will do a reprise on possible learnings.

In conclusion, for now, with questions to invite you into the process of reformulation, I offer a summary of ten seminal learnings that the church can mature into in conversation with jazz.

A Word about Fraser's Phraseology

I've been playing around with these ideas for at least 25 years. In that time, they have gone through many iterations and wordings. Over the next 20 years, my hope is that this will continue, that such improvisation in conversations within my networks will continue to illumine us in our reformulating of our understandings of our faith.

Friends often get exasperated with the way I use language. I cultivate those friendships, in part, precisely because of those exasperations. Many of those friends have worked this manuscript over and improved it greatly with their suggestions. But it is still riddled with "Fraserese." I hope that dialect, with its unique phraseology, will provoke for you new ways of seeing things. It's my approach, irritating at times even to me, to innovating with my languaging of my Canadian Presbyterian tradition in ways that make it more faithful, wise, and effective in my contribution to the missioning of Christ's church. My request is that you acknowledge and honor the irritations, then see if you can move beyond them to find a new perspective or conception in the words that sheds new light on your praxis of forgiving and reconciling love.

Engaging in Conversation with this Book

I can imagine a number of was of engaging in conversation with these prayers. I'll suggest a few:

- Just read them through as you would any book, resonating with what resonates and pondering what doesn't.
- Use each prayer as a weekly focus for your spiritual growth, noting what inspirations and insights arise in your considerations and figuring out how to play them with others.
- Convene some conversations about the prayers, read and considered in any mode you can imagine, in person or online, in any order you like.

You can probably imagine several others ways of entering into the swing of sanctifying significance I hope is generated by listening in on these conversations with the Spirit of our Creator's Christ, Jesus of Nazareth.

Thanks for Joining Me in the Dance Halls

I am convinced that the wit, wisdom, and workings of jazz offer seminal lessons for the church in how we might ally with God in redeeming the creation. This redeeming is a process of "sanctifying" that involves all of humanity in accepting the responsibilities assigned to us by our Creator in making things better. We are gifted with our "significance" as human beings by realizing the meaning of our lives in aligning with the workings of God in God's world and playing our unique gifts into the family business of caring for creation.

I'm currently imagining that family business, as mentioned, as a chain of dance halls. They are spaces where people find hospitality and companionship in an alienating and traumatizing world. They are places where the musicking of God's mercy and grace holds sway and cultivates sanctifying significance. They are places not well understood by those who look down on them from the outside. They are places where jazz reigns.

Thank you in anticipation for considering with me our sanctifying significance in conversation with the jazz community in the many manifestations of dance halls in our neighborhoods.

Brian Fraser
Easter 2026

Prelude

Imaging Lessons to Be Learned

Prayer 1

Dear Family of Creator, I have cut us off
from these morning times of conversation
for the past several weeks.

That now feels like a slothfulness of soul,
a suppressing of the significance of our friendship.
I lament and repent of the mornings lost,
resting in your forgiveness
and rejoicing in your reconciliation.

Your embrace is an elixir for my flourishing.
Your listening is a balm for my confusion.
Your wisdom is a light for my considerations.
Your companionship is life in all its fullness.

What I finally heard your stilling voice saying was
"Why don't we write that book you've been considering,
the one about what my church might learn from jazz,
in and through our prayerful conversations these mornings
and see how it all unfolds?"

What a provocative idea!
Let's do it.

These morning times together in our pandemic prayer diaries
have been the most fruitful and creatives times I have had for years.
You have enabled me to test out understandings of my faith,
ways of framing and phrasing them,
ways of recognizing how they are rooted
in the conversations that co-create the community of your church.

You have brought to mind the wisdom of Frank Barrett,
mentor in all things jazz and organizational
and a person of deepening faith,
when he said of jazz jams,
"Jazz musicians live for the jam sessions.
They love to play together, calling out songs for each other,
and then hang out afterward to talk about the session
and share experiences and insights.
A special kind of knowledge transfer takes place during those sessions,
one that cannot be replicated in any other way."[1]

So, I hope that these prayers will proceed in that teachable spirit.
I hope that you will enable me to recall
the voices of many who have inspired and instructed me in the faith.
I hope you will draw my attention to new conversation partners.
I hope those conversations and my reflections on them
will manifest a special kind of wisdom sharing
that nourishes souls to flourish in your mercy and grace.

All of these dynamics,
in the context of so many others undiscovered and unnamed,
awaken me more fully to my reliance on your resilience
in redeeming your world.

1. Barrett, *Yes*, 93.

[Appreciative inquiry] is a simple yet revolutionary philosophy of organizational learning and change: discover everything that "gives life" to the cooperative capacity of a human system—and then let go.

What gets co-constructed thereafter will be anything but linear. Like jazz improvisation or a creative jam session, it will literally be impossible to predict the emerging new opportunities, options, and shared possibilities. But one thing is almost certain: whatever gets created will be good. It will be valued and valuable to the human system for one overarching reason: the quality of the "relational space" from which the new constructions of the future are nurtured makes a difference that makes the difference.

Relationships . . . come alive where there is an appreciative question, when there is a deliberate search for the good and the best in one another; and in human systems the process of studying a phenomenon actually changes the phenomenon, in effect creating a new reality during the process of inquiry. That's what this book is all about. It is all about the power of "AI" as a way of creating a relational space for the cooperative construction of reality.[2]

2. Barrett and Fry, *Appreciative Inquiry*, 11.

Prayer 2

Dear Family of Creator, you draw us,
allure us, and attract us,
into the swing of your salvation.
It's an intriguing dynamic
that we will never understand fully
until we see you face-to-face
beyond all time and space
in the future you are fashioning
for the whole of your creation.

But you give us sufficient insight
into your aspirations for our emerging flourishing together
that we can use your gifts of consideration and choice
to ally ourselves with the melody, harmonies, and rhythms
of your commonwealth, your kinship,
as it breaks into our acedic present
from your rhapsodic future.

Awaken us to the signs of that future in our midst.

Draw our attention to the sociality of all that is,
most importantly you.
Draw our attention to the hope that infuses everything,
more and more convinced of it with every breath we take.

Draw our attention to the significance of all that we do,
so that the blessing you want us to offer happens.
Draw our attention to the awareness that deepens our grounding
in your faith, hope, and love.

Breath your mercy and grace on, in, and through us.

When musicians "hit the groove," they don't experience themselves as the source of that activity. This is ironic in a time when we put so much emphasis on autonomous skilled agents making rational, individual choices. When groups hit a groove, they talk about it as if the source of this activity comes from somewhere else. They apply masterful skillful activity and yet remain radically open to the surrounding situation that is calling forth a response. Musicians often speak of such moments in sacred metaphors: the beauty, the ecstasy, the divine, the transcendent joy, the spiritual dimension associated with being carried by a force larger than themselves.[3]

3. Barrett, *Yes*, 34.

Prayer 3

Dear Family of Creator, you suggested
that we pray the book first.
What a weird and wonderful approach
to reformulating my understanding of faith
as we explore what the church might learn from jazz!

The title is
What the Church Might Learn from Jazz:
Drawn into the Swing of Sanctifying Significance.

It all begins with your initiative.
Yours is the love that draws us together
into the community of interdependence that is your creation.
Your love is forgiving and reconciling.
It generates justice, kindness, and humility.
It provokes that kind of love for you, for others, and for ourselves.
It embraces us with a sense of how you created us to perform
as collegial contributors to your flourishing future.

There are levels of mystery in the dynamics of our relationship,
mystery in which you encounter us when we come together
in welcoming, worshiping, learning, and serving.
We humans will never understand that dynamic completely.
You call us to be a learning people with a teachable spirit

and to be satisfied enough with the levels of knowing
into which you draw us by the embrace of your love,
yet always being open to new learning.

It's an intriguing process of maturing
that we will never comprehend fully
until we see you face-to-face beyond all time and space.

But you reveal for us,
through the focal event
of your incarnation, crucifixion, resurrection, and ascension,
sufficient insight into your aspirations
for our emerging flourishing together.
You inspire and instruct us to use your gifts
of consideration, conversation, and choice
to ally ourselves with the melody, harmonies, and rhythms
of your commonwealth, your kinship,
as it breaks into our acedic present
from your rhapsodic future.

Somewhere deep in our souls
you have created an ability to respond
to your call for appreciative alliance with you
in caring for all of creation.
When you summon us to collaborate with you
in seeking the welfare of the world to which you have sent us,
we sense a significance being offered to us
that will nourish our flourishing.

We are invited to responsibility in contributing to a divine sociality
that encompasses past, present, and future generations.
This is the communion of saints to which we all belong

It is a community of your friends in Jesus Christ,
your church both manifest and latent,
who are working with you to compose themselves,
to the best of their abilities,
with the expressions of your flourishing
that emerge from the workings
of the mercy and grace of your Spirit—
love, joy, peace,
patience, kindness, generosity,
faithfulness, and gentleness.

Awaken us more fully to your summons
into such sanctifying significance.

I confess to a certain frustration that, when a constructive interest in improvisation is taken, attention often quickly focuses on preaching. Preaching is a vital aspect of worship, and it is an important practice in the shaping of the church. But to focus on the preacher as the one who improvises on the scriptural text is to miss two significant dimensions that this study seeks to highlight. One is that improvisation is not primarily about words: the first two practices I note, forming habits and assessing status, are not primarily cerebral or verbal practices. The second is that improvisation is a corporate activity: preaching always presupposes a period of corporate discernment and embodiment, which in most church services lasts little longer than the time it takes for the preacher to return to the stall. This study considers that process of corporate discernment and embodiment central to the mission and worship of the church.[4]

4. Wells, *Improvisation*, 18.

Prayer 4

Dear Family of Creator, one of the rich mysteries
into which you are drawing us
is the mystery of your swing.
As you embrace us with the swing of your mercy and grace,
we are drawn into your intermingling dance of all creation.

Louis Armstrong once said of jazz
that if you have to ask what it means
then you don't really get it.
The same is often said of swing.

But that has not stopped generations of musicians
from trying to put it into words.
Nor has it stopped me from trying
to make clear sense of those efforts
and use it as an analogy
for your ways of generating sanctifying significance.

Swing is a form of musicking
that draws you into dancing.
Its rhythms resonate deeply in our human soul
to get us moving forward together in joyful sync.

Here are some of the phrases I've heard used
to point to this dynamic:

- playing that has a strong groove or drive;
- innovative arrangements that feature call and response;
- freedom for soloists to create melodic lines;
- uplifting for body and soul;
- an irresistible gravitational buoyancy that defies mere verbal definition;
- you can feel it, but you just can't explain it;
- rhythmic coordination that commands a visceral response;
- a compelling momentum that results from attacks and accents;
- swing remains indefinable;
- a rhythmical property that conveys some kind of forward movement;
- a mixture of an underlying regular pulse with minute variations of that pulse;
- an ongoing natural flow;
- dance music that is simple with clear melodies and strong beats;
- normally played by big bands;
- musicians playing off each other's musical inspirations in the moment;
- approach playing together with a fresh and invigorating spirit, and respond to each other with daring and joy;
- a hybrid of time/pulse and rhythm;
- the result of a mixing of triple metre and multiple rhythmic layering with Western European duple metre and singular rhythm developed throughout the African diaspora;
- marked by methodical improvisation, quick tempos, and rambunctiousness; and

- ultimately [swing] depends on the interplay of numerous factors, ranging from the sheer variety of the artists' rhythmic conception to the stylistic manner in which they articulate and phrase them, imbuing them with the qualities of syncopation and forward motion.

Let us, then, draw our own analogy between swing and faith
as you have revealed it in these attempts to name the undefinable.

There is a resonant rhythmic impulse in swing
that compels us to move forward in a syncopated togetherness.

There is an irresistible buoyancy in swing
that inspires daring and joy,
a boisterous, delighted participation,
in the interdependencies of the musicking.

There is a myriad of influences that flow together in swing
that trace their roots back through the African diaspora
to the primal spiritualities of your peoples in those places.

There is a mingling of styles, mannerisms, and phrasings in swing
as your ambassadors appropriate their unique composings
of the hope that flows from your forgiving and reconciling love.

In the end, swing is all of this and more,
a mysterious energy that reveals clear and compelling insights
into the astounding and confounding ways
that you transform the dance of flourishing
for which you have created us.

[A] joy of jazz is the elusive concept of swing. Most fans know when it's there (or isn't), but it is quite difficult to define in words. . . . [When listening to jazz], ask yourself whether it moves you, outwardly or inwardly, to want to swing and dance. If not, then it may not be real jazz.[5]

5. Edgar, *Supreme Love*, 176–77.

Prayer 5

Dear Family of Creator, you desire to sanctify your whole creation,
including and especially we human beings.
You have given us a special degree of responsibility
for imagining, composing, and performing
the swing of sanctification
that will bless the whole world.

We are endowed by you through being created
with the capacities to bless each other
in the places to which you have summoned us
to partner with you in nourishing flourishing life.

We are equipped by you with the tools to bless this world,
tools to be used in expanding the family business
of caring for your creation.
You sanctify this earth, our family home,
by bringing into our present
the future you have fashioned for your universe.
It swings to the redemptive melodies and harmonies of
love, joy, peace, patience, kindness, generosity,
faithfulness, and gentleness,
all composed with us into a divine dance
of delightful forgiveness and reconciliation.

We are educated by you through companionship with you
to bring us into alliance with you
in doing what you desire—
be just, be kind, be humble in walking with you
to the beat of your drumming.

We are empowered by you to be ambassadors
of your work for your world.
The capacities with which you endowed us,
the tools with which you equipped us,
the alliance for which you educated us,
all flow together into the swing of sanctification
that gives us our significance
in the coming of your commonwealth.

But we have rebelled in arrogant antagonism to your summons.

Listen,
in your forgiving and reconciling love,
to our confession.
Inspire in us a level of sanctifying honesty
by your assurance of our unconditional belonging
to your communion of saints
who you have redeemed for serving your flourishing future
over all generations.

We have assumed that we can know more than we do,
especially when it comes to good and evil.
Family of Creator, have mercy.

We have assumed that we can control more than we can,
especially when it comes to manipulating your creation.
Family of Creator, have mercy.

We have assumed that we are
your only chosen people,
especially when it comes to dominating others.
Family of Creator, have mercy.

We have assumed that we can know your will,
especially when it comes to organizing our life together.
Family of Creator, have mercy.

We have assumed that we are separate and special,
selected out from others for your favors,
especially when it comes to possessions and privilege.
Family of Creator, have mercy.

In our fearful obsession with protecting our fortunes,
we have cut ourselves off from you
and all the true sources of flourishing that you have provided.
We have become stuck in thickets of trauma
too complicated and constricting
to get out of alone.
The music of our lives is a dirge,
focused too exclusively on dread, destruction, and death.

But in that lament, dear Family of Creator,
in the midst of oppression and exploitation,
of sinning and being sinned against,
from the cross of ignominy and shame,

the sounds of your forgiving and reconciling swing can be heard,
a still, small voice at first, perhaps,
summoning us to a different way of being with you,
a way that provokes us into significance
in sanctifying your creation.

The story of jazz, collective and personal, is always in formation. Jazz forms and re-forms itself. Usually, it is the deliberate intention of the jazz artist to play the old story in new ways, or play a new story in the open space of freedom, the spiritual quintessential element of jazz. This new story is informed by the collective story of triumph and tragedy, the personal story of composition and interpretation, and the artist's own trudging and soaring imaginings.[6]

6. Jones, *Jazz of Preaching*, 35.

Prayer 6

Dear Family of Creator, your sanctifying work
arises from your promise to bless all of your creation.
You have included us in a special way in that desire.
You have given us a special degree of responsibility
when it comes to the kinship and interdependency
that you wish to see on your beloved earth.

As we consider what it means for us
to participate in and contribute to
the fuller realization of your forgiveness and reconciliation,
we review with regret the many ways
in which our communal understanding
has misrepresented the purpose, promises, and processes
involved the sanctifying work you invite us to undertake with you.

One of the greatest distortions we have perpetuated
is the idea that sanctification
has to do with us as individuals.
It is about us getting your holiness for ourselves,
about us becoming purified from our personal sinfulness.
It has to do with our anxieties about our status.
We look to you for assurances that we are OK,
saved into a special status that sets us apart and above,

associating and assembling with those who are like us
for mutual support in our privilege.

But sanctifying has to do with the healing and wholeness
of your creation.
You created us to be partners with you in that enterprise.
In Jesus, your Christ, you have fulfilled your promise
that you align and ally us with your family business.

You are inviting us into a redeeming process
by provoking us to see things differently.
Through a myriad of means,
inspirations and influences that come to us
from within and from outside your manifest church,
you constantly reformulate our understandings of your faith in us
and of our trust in and loyalty to your desire
to see everything work together
for justice,
in kindness,
with humility in working together with you.

Your sense of wholeness,
as you have revealed it to us in Jesus, your Christ,
embraces the well-being of all creation
in a dance of delight
over the flourishing of your communion of the sanctified.

Help us accept, appreciate, and apply this gift of belonging.

Who is man? A being in travail with God's dreams and designs, with God's dream of a world redeemed, of reconciliation of heaven and earth, of a mankind that is truly His image, reflecting His wisdom, justice, and compassion. God's dream is not to be alone, to have mankind as a partner in the drama of continuous creation. By whatever we do, by every act we carry out, we either advance or obstruct the drama of redemption; we either reduce or enhance the power of evil.[7]

7. Heschel, *What Is Man?*, 119.

Prayer 7

Dear Family of Creator, I'm sitting in prayer with you,
just in front of the back fence
at the Kaslo Jazz Etc. Summer Music Festival.
I'm people watching and wondering.

They cover the ground,
line up patiently in good humour for hours at the food trucks,
greet friends (and maybe strangers) with abandon and appreciation,
dance, applaud, shout,
in all shapes, sizes, ages, genders, and races,
clad, to varying degrees, in all manner of dress.

Amidst this congregation of your human creations,
is there anything that you are doing
to reveal your intention to them?

Is there something in their gratitude and geniality
that is generated by your mercy and grace?

Is there something in their delight in diversity
that arises from the flourishing of resilient life that you sustain?

Is there something in their resonance
with the sound and substance of the musicking

that awakens them to the possibility
that this kind of communing is a gift flowing from you?

They will not be with us worshiping
in the little United Church here in Kaslo tomorrow morning.

They do not recognize your agency among them
in any ways familiar to most of us
who identify as Christians through the institutional church.

Is there something you want us to learn
from the lively sense of togetherness
manifest at this festival?
Is this part of your "invisible" church
to which you are inviting us to listen
and from whom you are inviting us to learn?

And the New Orleans brass band on the floating stage
has just burst into "When the saints."
Everybody is singing along!

What significance do the saints
I'm watching and wondering about
find in this festival?

How are you using that significance
to sanctify your world?

How can we in your manifest church
unlearn the ways we have misrepresented you for generations
and learn anew the ways you are working among

these siblings of ours that you call upon us to bless
with abundant opportunities to flourish
as you desire for all of us so deeply?

As you inspire the composition of this prayer book,
keep me alert to all those who share in your workings and wisdom
through their delight in the life you have given them.

The freedom to develop faithful communities in a particular context actually can allow people to find meaningful connection with wider traditions, both those belonging to the Christian faith and those of the community's ancestors or neighbors who were not Christians. In them, the community can learn to discern the healing, transformative work of the Spirit. . . . [For the Galatians, this] opened the door for much creativity and locally based solutions about how to follow Jesus in a given place and time. Any given culture will have both liberating and oppressive aspects that need to be deepened or transformed, as the case may be.[8]

8. Bedford, *Galatians*, 8–9.

Prayer 8

Dear Family of Creator, what significance
have you entrusted to your human creatures?
You have entrusted us with a special degree of responsibility
for contributing the abilities you have given us
to caring for your creation and its flourishing evolution.

These capabilities you have bestowed upon us
give us value and worth,
import and weight,
dignity and influence,
attention and meaning,
importance and consequence.

All of these qualities of relating
arise from and are sustained by
the life-giving dynamics that you generate
among us and within us
in every breath we take.
Whether we recognize and appreciate this or not,
you are always offering it.
These are the workings that animate your church,
both manifest and latent, visible and invisible,
with all of its potential for contributing to the full realization
of the kinship offered in your communion of saints.

Maybe that's the wording that resonates more truly
as we seek to language the world of our relating
that you are remaking for your benefit and ours.
You are inviting, inspiring, instructing us
to become more fully your community of sanctifiers.

Especially in the Western Christian traditions,
we have distorted our representations of you
through the use of imperial and monarchical authoritarian language—
kingdom, majesty, lord, rule, obedience, high priest, even shepherd.
All have positive resonance with care, when practiced well.
But all also have negative connotations
of power over, of inflicting subjugation, of imposing subservience,
often accompanied by the use of violence.
When we represent you in such imperious ways,
we seek to survive through compliance and conformity.
We become pawns in a game of conquest and control,
soldiers in wars of good against evil.

We seek survival in a hostile world through frenzied assault.
We are caught up in self-righteous fear for survival,
too lazy to consider different ways of being significant,
ways that align and ally
with your comprehensive and inclusive communion of saints.

And we enlist you as our supreme champion,
our David against the Goliath
of whoever we have decided to hate in our fears and fantasies.
The corrosive complications of this way of being together
compound over the generations.
We delude ourselves that this is the way you want things to be,

your servants doing your will to defeat your enemies
through vitriol and violence until the final victory is yours.

There is none of the significance
with which you endowed and entrusted to us.
Help us relearn how to represent you
faithfully, wisely, and effectively.

Musicians cannot become deep souls without emptying themselves, without losing themselves in music that lives by the virtues of honesty, vitality, and freedom. As they surrender their will to the creative process, they lay their souls open to be shaped by grace. It is analogous to any other repeated activity in life. The more you practice it, the more it shapes you.[9]

9. Carter, *Thriving*, 164

Prayer 9

Dear Family of Creator, this is my introductory sense
of what I understand to be your purpose and processes
of drawing us into the swing of sanctifying significance.

It is a responsibility entrusted to us by you
to compose ourselves in conscious companionship with you
so that we live together with the whole of your creation
in love, joy, peace, patience, kindness, generosity,
faithfulness, and gentleness.

You model those virtues for us in Jesus of Nazareth,
your Christ in whom you took our human flesh fully
and identified with us so we could identify with you.
This mysterious yet meaningful sanctification of us
into your communion of saints
who are ambassadors of your message of forgiving and reconciling love
is the swing of our betterment.

Help us find in our explorations of your workings
in the dynamics of the jazz community
ways of reformulating our understanding of your revelation
about how to be partners with you in your care for your creation.

You have always sought to play to our teachable spirit.
You have always pestered us and provoked us
with permissions to compose new possibilities
for realizing more fully our responsibilities
in playing your Redemption Suite.
As players in your band,
blend our performances to express your mercy and grace.

It is in relation to the life of the triune God being a partnership that the metaphor of the dance seems particularly apropos. . . . The God who made us did not leave us to manage on our own, but gives us our breath and our life, new every moment. The dance goes on; creation continues. The God who redeemed us continues working to "conform us to the image of the Son"—a spiritual process often known as sanctification.[10]

10. Rigby, *Holding Faith*, 135–36.

Prayer 10

Dear Family of Creator, you know better than us
that all jazz is not swing and all swing is not jazz.
In a similar way, all church is not faithful, wise, and effective
and all that is faithful, wise, and effective is not church.
Your ambassadors in this realm and this time
are all treasures in earthen vessels,
whether they identify as church or not.
Your communion of sanctifiers is both manifest and latent.

This exploration of your redemptive relationship
with your human family
seeks to listen with respect
to all the voices through whom you continue
to draw us into the empathy, courage, and resilience
that will transform our life together for the better.

Much gets in the way of this happening
in our current darkness.

Much arises that prevents us from fully participating and contributing.

Much is generated by our fear, laziness, and self-righteousness
that diminishes our ability to ally with you

and realize the possibilities offered
to and through your community of sanctifiers in your world.

Awaken us to the meanings you are revealing
in the mysteries of our disciplines
in maturing in our ambassadorship for your commonweal.

In this book, I address the challenges of these dark times to help us restore to our house a spiritual foundation of courage, strength, self-reflection, creativity, compassion, and faith. These are not conservative values or progressive ones, not Democratic or Republican. They are deeply spiritual values that should unnerve both "sides." The binary, two-party frame of our political system is too small to contain the vast, wondrous nature of these ideals. Through these values, we learn to face and make spiritual use of our fear, anger, confusion, chaos, and all the other challenges of our political and spiritual midnight. We can rediscover the superheroes hidden within each of us and work to build the nation for which we yearn. We can find the spiritual resistance and spiritual resilience that it will take.[11]

11. Moss, *Dancing*, 7.

Prayer 11

Dear Family of Creator, let's explore some of the dynamics
that drag our attention away from your sanctifying work in your world.
You are patiently and persistently drawing our attention
to the light of your justice, your kindness, and your humility,
to the purity of your peace.

But we stay stuck in the shadows
of our arrogant wager that we can do life well without you.
There is a stifling shame there that arises from our feelings
of not being the selves you created us to be.
We often think of this in terms of being judged by you,
of being brought to shame by your condemnation of our sinful selves.
We impose our truncated understandings of judgement on you
and feel condemned, deserving of punishment, shunned,
despised and rejected, devoid of all dignity and worth.

Yet that is how you came to be with us and for us in Jesus,
hanging around with shamed people,
acting in ways that led the authorities of that day
to attempt to shame you
with all the indignities associated with execution.
The people you hung around with,
much like us in our day,
internalized that shame into feelings of insignificance.

Many of us became silent, invisible, submissive, and servile.
Some of us usurped the right to define good and evil
in ways that imposed a tyrannical order
on the creation you made to be interdependent
in right relationships modeled on your justice and your peace.

You took our insignificance into the very marrow of your bones,
into the very essence of your humanity
where your life-giving energy generates our flourishing.
You transformed it into significance in your commonweal
where everyone has a constructive contribution to make.
The dynamics of that transformation are veiled in mystery.
The impact of that transformation
on our ways of showing up with others
for justice, with kindness, and in humility
reveals the purpose and power of your mercy and grace.

Modern researchers have come to understand shame
as the intensely painful feeling
of believing we are flawed in our very essence
and therefore unworthy of love and belonging.
Shame is the fear of disconnection,
the lethargy that prevents us from forging bonds,
and the self-righteousness that deludes us
into hiding our sense of failure in an insistence on superiority.
It is a profound sense that we are bad to the very core of our beings.
It corrupts our relationship with you and others
and disintegrates all the capabilities that generate vision and creativity
to provoke goodness, beauty, and joy
in the lives of others.

In Jesus, you Christify our sense of ourselves
so we can mature into appreciating the unconditional acceptance
that you alone can provide.
In that confidence, we grow into your calling into our true identity.

Shatter the husks of our shame
with the sanctifying significance you have sown within us.

One way to approach [shame's] essence is to understand it as an undercurrent of sensed emotion, of which we have either a slight or robust impression that, should we put it into words, would declare some version of I am not enough; there is something wrong with me; I am bad; I don't matter. . . . by shame, I am not talking about something that necessarily requires the intensity of extreme humiliation. Rather, it is born of a sense of "there being something wrong" with me or of "not being enough," and therefore exudes an aroma of being unable or powerless to change one's condition or circumstances.[12]

12. Thompson, *Soul*, 24.

Prayer 12

Dear Family of Creator, where do you shatter those husks of shame?
You have chosen four communal disciplines
through which you take a special degree of responsibility
for healing your people into hopefulness.

The discipline of welcoming the world
into a realization that they belong in your kinship
is called *koinonia*.

The discipline of worshiping in gratitude
for that welcoming mercy and grace
is called *liturgia*.

The discipline of learning more fully
the providential possibilities
that your forgiveness and reconciliation provoke
is called *didache* of the *kerygma*.

The discipline of serving your commonweal
that you are bringing to us from your flourishing future
is called *diakonia*.

Indeed, it is through these traditional disciplines of your church—
koinonia, liturgia, didache, kerygma, and diakonia—

that you reveal enough of your mysterious workings
to enable us to co-compose ourselves with you
into a company of ambassadors for your forgiven and reconciled world.

In each of these communal practices,
you work among us and within us
to bring us to a fuller realization
of the gift of joyful relationship with you
that empowers us to care for your creation.

Awaken us to your provocations to love and good works
in all of the engagements you generate in our lives.

The Psalms are a rich read for all sorts of reasons. They're beautiful, sophisticated poetry, for one. They also have catechetical purposes, teaching the stories *of* God's people *to* God's people, in ways they can recall together again and again. The Psalms craft powerful, creative metaphors, like God as a sheltering bird under hose wings one can find refuge (Psalm 91). But one of the psalm's greatest gifts—one certainly not lost on Fred [Rogers]—is the vast range of human emotion and experience they represent. While there are psalms of pure praise, brimming with joy and worship of God (for example, Psalm 150), many more psalms give voice to feelings of loneliness (Psalm 88), fear (Psalm 22), grief (Psalm 6), and anger (Psalm 137)—right along side their verses of praise.

. . . The content of the psalms indicates that God and God's people have blessed emotional expression of thousands of years. Fred heard that cue and joined the song.[13]

13. Tuttle. *Exactly*, 32.

Prayer 13

Dear Family of Creator, when you enhanced your sanctifying work
in Jesus, your Messiah and Christ,
you freed us from the strictures of the "shoulds"
that some self-proclaimed authorities imposed on our lives.
Granted, we are all too willing to accept those strictures
in our fearfulness and laziness.
We find security, acceptance, and power
in perpetuating and propagating these limitations
as the way things must be
in our closed order of creation.
We bind ourselves to a stifling significance
as guardians of our misrepresentations of your will.

That is not the significance you want for us.

Your self-disclosure in Jesus of Nazareth
awakens us to the "coulds"
designed by you to enable us to ally with you
in bringing about the flourishing open future you are creating.

In that work, we come to ourselves
and realize that our true identity
lies in companionship with you

in co-creating the coming commonweal of your creation.
Our sanctifying significance lies in allying with your saving work.

You drew us into a world of promises fulfilled,
purpose clarified, possibilities opened,
provocations appreciated, and processes suggested.

There is a swing at play in that world.
It was shaped and reshaped by
the dynamics of your forgiving and reconciling love
revealed most fully and fruitfully
in the ways you manifested your image in us
in Jesus of Nazareth.

You invite us, inspire us, persuade us, redeem us,
into a simple rhythm of grace and gratitude
that pulses with sanctifying significance
for the welfare of your world,
that energizes our bodies and souls
in your dance of devoted mutual delight
in the flourishing future we are creating together.

Stir our souls with the swing
of your justice, kindness, and humility.

I believe Christian thinking and social witness can be understood analogically with jazz music. Like jazz, Christianity is a dramatic and musical performance. Like jazz, Christian thinking and acting are improvisational, creative, and hopefully forward looking. Like jazz, they exemplify a dynamic of constraint and possibility. Constrained by the norm of God's Word, Christians seek to creatively engage their world in light of the Word. In their work and witness, Christians use the materials at hand—principally the language and example of the prophets and Jesus in the context of their life—to creatively riff for justice, love, and shalom in the present and thereby open us to a new future.[14]

14. Heltzel, *Resurrection City*, 21.

Prayer 14

Dear Family of Creator, you offer us space
that is sufficiently safe for us
to surrender our suffering and shame to you in lament
in the sure knowledge that we will heal through your hope.

That is a space where you (*theos*)
gather us in relationship as your beloved (*logos*),
where our theology is composed and improvised,
where we belong because you have forgiven and reconciled us,
where we are welcomed home with unconditional hospitality.

In that sacred space where you embrace us,
wherever that place of mercy and grace may be,
our redemption continues with a dance of delight.

That dance is part of the "musicking"
that fills your world with your providential playfulness.
It happens through life-giving networks of interdependencies.
The intricacies and complexities of these networks
are beyond our comprehension.

We rely on you to compose
the friendly workings of your creation

in ways that resonate
with our sanctifying significance as partners with you.

We rely on you to arrange us
so we synchronize with you and others
as we contribute ever more consciously and constructively
to the flourishing of your commonweal.

All of humanity is your jazz band.
We are your instrument.

All of creation is your audience in your divine dance hall.

Your sanctifying swing gives us all our delightful significance.

> The fundamental nature and meaning of music lie not in objects, not in musical works at all, but in action, in what people do. It is only by understanding what people do as they take part in a musical act that we can hope to understand its nature and the function it fulfills in human life. Whatever that function may be, I am certain, first, that to take part in a music act is of central importance to our very humanness, as important as taking part in the act of speech, which it so resembles (but from which it also differs in important ways), and second, that everyone, every normally endowed human being, is born with the gift of music no less than with the gift of speech. . . . This book, then, is not so much about music as it is about people, about people as they play and sing, as they listen and compose, and even as they dance (for in many cultures if no one is dancing then no music is happening, so integral is dance to the musical act), and about the ways they—we—go about singing and playing and composing and listening. It is also about the reasons we feel the urge to do these things and why we feel good when we do them well. We could say it is not so much about music as it is about people musicking.[15]

15. Small, *Musicking*, 8–9.

Prayer 15

Dear Family of Creator, we too often see Sabbath
as rest from things that cause us stress and suffering,
particularly from the work that we do.
It's an understanding that focuses on us and what we are doing.
It's an understanding that narrows in on the benefits to us.
It's an understanding that distorts the dynamic you intend.

What if we shifted and broadened our focus?
What if we began to see Sabbath as rest in you
rather than rest from something?
What would happen in that resting?

First and foremost, you would have our attention.
Your Sabbath would be a time in our relationship
when we take special heed of the mutual benefit
we enjoy in our friendship,
a friendship started, shaped, and sustained by your promise
of a flourishing and fruitful life together.
In the traditions that have grown from that kind of belonging,
we call it "covenant."

Resting in you in Sabbath is a time to renew that covenant.
It is a time to remember your forgiveness and reconciliation
amid our ongoing rebellions.

It is you who invite and welcome us into Sabbath,
not us who decide to take a Sabbath.

On this Sabbath, guide our interactions
in ways that nourish us to flourish in your mercy and grace.

Jazz is neither free improvisation, nor a faithful hewing to the tradition, but a hybrid of the two. Speaking with the form and giving it a new voice.[16]

16. Nachmanovich, *Art*, 92

Prayer 16

Dear Family of Creator, the companionship that you nourish
in your Sabbath times
inspires and instructs us as your ambassadors.
That summons to a sanctifying significance
is the core chart of our identity and vocation.
It is your Spirit's call inviting our response.
The primal rhythm pulsing through it
is grace and gratitude,
your grace provoking our gratitude.
That is our dance of mutual devotion and delight.

Throughout the biblical records,
we are made aware of you have forgiven and reconciled us
after our ancestors
decided to live without relating humbly with you
and later generations compounded
the traumas of that rebellion.
You never gave up on us.
You never ceased to invite us home
from our wanton wanderings
and to find our sanctifying significance
in caring for your creation as stewards of your SHALOM.

In spite of our ongoing rebellion and its consequences,
that invitation to the dance of your delight stands.

Draw us into your devotion to our sanctifying significance.

I will sing a new song. As difficult as it is, I must learn the new song that is capable of meeting the new need. I must fashion new words born of all the new growth of my life, my mind and my spirit. I must prepare for new melodies that have never been mine before, that all that is within me may lift my voice unto God. How I love the old familiarity of the wearied melody—how I shrink from the harsh discords of the new untried harmonies.

Teach me, my Father, that I might learn with the abandonment and enthusiasm of Jesus, the fresh new accent, the untried melody, to meet the need of the untried morrow. Thus, I may rejoice with each new day and delight my spirit in each fresh unfolding. I will sing, this day, a new song unto Thee, O God.[17]

17. Thurman, *Meditations*, 206–7.

Prayer 17

Dear Family of Creator, as ways of alluring and attracting us
into your dance of hospitality, hope, and healing,
you use a myriad of methods,
many of them involving musicking.
You seek to awaken our whole beings
to the dynamics of your mercy and grace,
to set up the vibe of grace and gratitude
that energizes us for sanctifying significance.
That vibe is in our very bones, in our DNA,
because you sowed it there in our creation.
It is your image in us.
It is your energy that gives us the life of your self-giving love.

Mysterious as your workings are so often,
you have given us the capabilities to sense our need for belonging,
for connections that cultivate constructive contributions
to the care of your creation.
Musicking is often the method you use to activate that sense.

Jazz is not for everyone.
But you have been generating connections
in and through Brentwood Presbyterian Church in Burnaby, BC,
that are forming networks of nourishment

in maturing to the fullness of flourishing
that you seek to provoke in all humankind.

As we compose these devotional dialogues,
draw forth from them sanctifying lessons
your church might learn from jazz.

> All the skills which . . . should characterize the Church as persons-in-communion . . . are present in a very heightened form [in jazz improvisation]: giving 'space' to the other through alert attentiveness, listening in patient silence, contributing to the growth of others by 'making the best' of what is received from them so they are encouraged to continue participating, sensitive decision-making, flexibility of response, initiating change, role-changing, generating and benefiting from conflict.[18]

18. Begbie, *Theology*, 206.

Prayer 18

Dear Family of Creator, what if
we imagine these devotional dialogues as a jazz suite,
composed in words rather than musical notes,
that bring together the dance tunes you have taught us
over the past seventy-nine years of friendship?

What if we imagined three movements?

The first movement
might focus on the transcendent dynamic of your call
that jazz musicians sense and express in their lives.
They see themselves composing and playing love stories
that proceed from and are sustained by a spiritual energy
that invites their response
and drives their creativity and its expression.

They give voice to the joys and sorrows of our relationships
in profound expressions of the intuitions, emotions, and ideas
that are integrated into wisdom in the human soul.

They hone the substance and sound of their musicking
by hanging out with each other,
playing and pondering the possibilities that emerge
as the conversations explore the dynamics of their connecting.

Their comprehension and articulation of their spiritualities,
like their compositions and performances of their music,
are delightfully hybrid in both sources and expressions.

In all of this curiosity, creativity, and collaboration,
where to we detect your redemptive workings?
Where do we discover the pervasive influences
of your desire to draw all humankind
back into relationship with you and all your kin
in the care of your creation?
Where do we discern your forgiving and reconciling love
working its wonders of hospitality, hope, and healing?
Where does the manifest church find
in the latent church among the jazz community
inspiration and insights to reformulate its missioning
in ways that represent you more faithfully, wisely, and effectively?

You have shown us in Jesus, your Christ,
how the power of your Presence is at work in your world.
The whole of the Hebrew and Christian scriptures
bear witness to the dynamics of how you use your power.
It shows up in the fruits of your Spirit at work
in the places and ways you choose,
in love, joy, peace, patience, kindness, generosity,
faithfulness and gentleness,
all composed into selves maturing in you
to contribute to your future realization of your commonweal
as it disrupts the grunge and grime
of our current ways of living together.

Where in jazz can we find you engaged in that work?

How are you expressing yourself in jazz
to draw us into your love dance?

The second movement
might focus on the companionship you offer
through the rhythms of grace and gratitude
to bring us into sync with your community of sanctifiers.
You have encouraged us to provoke one another
to love and good deeds.
You always remind us
that this is best done in conscious relationship with you
as we are nourished to flourish in the communal disciplines
of your manifest church.
You also make it clear
that we flourish most fully
as ambassadors of your mercy and grace,
as provocateurs of your forgiveness and reconciliation.

We might tell stories from the jazz community
about its roots in your gospel's impact on people
in the midst of the tumult and trauma of slavery
and about the continuing racism that denies belonging
to peoples who did not fit into distorted definitions of good.

We might remember,
prompted by the primal resilience of the jazz community,
what your vision for the future of your world really is.

We might imagine improvising our lives around this vision,
working together in concert
one conversation after another

as we co-create with you and each other
better ways of living together in justice, kindness, and humility.

The third movement
might focus on your inspirations and instructions
for living into the new humanity you inaugurated in Jesus Christ
by making practical changes in the tunes we are playing right now
and the ways we are playing them.

We might imagine how the manifest church would be reformed
if we took the dynamics of jazz as a model of missioning
for your kingdom, your kinship, your commonweal
in the neighborhoods where you have planted us.

We might explore more boldly the freedom you give us
to change for the better
in order to contribute more consciously
to our family business of caring for creation.

We might be awakened to the sanctifying significance
you have sown in all of us
so that we mature into responsible members of your body
that is bringing in your desired future for your beloved world.

To conclude the suite
we might reprise the soul of our significance
that you have revealed to us through these discerning dialogues
with the wit, wisdom, and workings of jazz.

We'll do that in the form of questions,
drawing on the kind of curiosity
that generates the swing of great jazz.

By your mercy and grace, the beat goes on
in the divine dance hall of your creation.

The conservatism of jazz derives from the fact that the ancestors are always with us on the bandstand, revealing themselves in the various ways in which they have influenced and shaped the voices and the aesthetic sensibilities of musicians as they contribute to the emerging conversation. The progressivism of jazz derives from the fact that these conversations are improvised and involve taking something familiar and discovering a new way of "talking" about it. . . . While the ancestors have taught us the language and the vocabulary of jazz, we honor them, not by copying and repeating what they said, but by using that language and vocabulary to go places they haven't been.[19]

19. Hayman, *Tale*, 129.

First Movement

Considering God's Call

Prayer 19

Dear Family of Creator, you encourage us insistently
to stay focused on the fact that this whole enterprise of being church
proceeds from and is sustained by
your determination to save your world.

You have created us to be partners in that family business.
You have gifted us with capabilities to contribute to it.
You have opened up possibilities for us
to play justice with kindness in humility.

Awaken us more fully in these devotions
to that sanctifying significance.

Keep us mindful that you are always with us in this enterprise,
calming our fears, provoking our curiosity,
and making us appreciative of the potential you are generating.

Spark our imaginations with the dynamics of your workings
in and through the jazz community.

Infuse all of our missioning in all of our networks
with the resilient resonance of generations of jazz musicians
who have found in that art form
hospitality, hope, and healing.

The dance that is jazz bears all the marks of your gospel—
welcoming, worshiping, learning, and serving.

The forms and formulations that those practices of your church take
in the dance halls and jazz clubs and house concerts and jams
may not seem true to you on first glance,
but open our eyes and ears that we may see and hear
your latent church flowing in a musicking
that provides belonging, blessing, and benefits for all involved.

Hone your gifts of loitering, listening, and learning in us
to guide us into a fascinating series of conversations
that might open up for us new perspectives
on how you are bringing your flourishing future
into our tumultuous present to heal our traumatizing past.

Because of your pervasive Presence in your beloved world,
it is not only in the manifest church
that we can find little schools of faith.
Among the many places your gospel is flourishing
are the spaces of grace in which jazz happens.
Attune us to that possibility.

A quantum organization would be like a jazz jam session. . . . [It would] create infrastructures where different questions can be asked, different goals considered, different products or functions imagined. Roles would be less fixed, employees encouraged to play different instruments and to experiment with the score. A quantum leader would see himself holding the space where the background theme can emerge. Quantum selves are designed to thrive at the edge. A quantum organization would have some infrastructure that allows for the free play of uncertainty.[20]

20. Zohar, *Rewiring,* 126.

Prayer 20

Dear Family of Creator, you caught my attention this morning
with wording that Paul used in writing to the Corinthian church
that I have not considered carefully before.
You used, of all things, a Stephen King novel, *Revival*.
The wording, in the New American Standard Bible translation, is:

". . . now I know in part, but then I will know fully
just as I also have been fully known."[21]

What startled me was the reminder
that all of this praying is really an exploration
in conversation with you
about how you fully know me in your love.
That is the foundation for the sanctifying significance
you summon me to assume
in your family dance hall business
as we collaborate in inviting the demeaned and the dismissed
into gatherings of hospitality, hope, and healing.

That knowing love is seen most clearly
in the ways you showed up
in the midst of the mess that existed in Galilee

21. First Corinthians 13:12b (NAB).

during your human life on this earth
in Jesus of Nazareth.

It is also seen embodied in the love of Mary, his mother.
It is a love that grew as she nurtured him to birth
and to a deep internalization of
the best traditions of your servant people, Israel.
The depths to which that tradition had shaped Mary
are expressed eloquently in the Magnificat,
her exuberant hymn of praise to you during her pregnancy:

"My soul proclaims your greatness, O God,
and my spirit rejoices in you, my Savior.
For you have looked with favor upon your lowly servant,
and from this day forward all generations will call me blessed.
For you, the Almighty, have done great things for me;
and holy is your Name.
Your mercy reaches from age to age for those who fear you.
You have shown your strength with your arm;
you have scattered the proud in their conceit;
you have deposed the mighty from their thrones
and raised the lowly to high places.
You have filled the hungry with good things,
while you have sent the rich away empty.
You have come to the aid of Israel, your servant,
mindful of your mercy—
the promise you made to our ancestors—
to Sarah and Abraham
and their descendants forever."[22]

22. Luke 1:46b–55 (IB).

You know our rebellions against our responsibilities
better than we do,
yet you persist in provoking us to partner with you.
You draw us into knowing you and ourselves more deeply
in Mary's exultant song of praise
to the redemptive work you are doing in your world
for the sake of its flourishing.

The things you pay attention to in this song of your salvation
show us how to listen and learn
as we mature in our own faithfulness, wisdom, and effectiveness.
They are the messages of the prophetic traditions
which Jesus lived and taught with a singular devotion.
They are the attitudes and behaviors that you compose
into the suites of sanctifying significance
that you are inviting us to play with you
for the welfare of your whole creation.

You enjoy being praised for your steadfast love.
You endow your humble servants
with the capabilities of being a blessing
that inspires and influences multiple generations.
You continue to work your redemption over the generations
in spite of the resistance and indifference
of your beloved humans.
That new way of living together
will be characterized by a humble mutuality
in the distribution of power and possessions.
All of this proceeds from your covenant with Abraham and Sarah
that you will be our God so we can bless your creation.

You have created us to be ambassadors
of this kind of forgiving and reconciling love
in all of the networks in which you intend us
to have sanctifying significance.

Guide our discernment
as we explore the ways Mary's depth of faith
can be discerned in both your manifest and latent churches,
where we are encountered by the swing of your salvation
in your dance halls.

Open up for us
the knowledge of your mercy and grace
that you have sown in the jazz community,
earthen as that vessel may be
in expressing your treasure.

Remind us in these conversations
that your manifest church
is no less earthen than your latent church.

Jazz was born out of a time of great cultural and social change. It emerged out of sorrow, fear and hope. It developed as old patterns of life were being, sometimes unsuccessfully, challenged. The brew of the knowing and the unknowing, the experience and the challenges of a changing paradigm can all be felt in jazz music. But it is also felt in the church today. As we have already considered, we live in a time of great uncertainty. It is a time when many of our old certainties are being challenged by new cultural questions. It may be a time of fear, sorrow and hope for all of us and it is a time into which the metaphor of jazz speaks.[23]

23. Drummond, *All That Jazz*, 25.

Prayer 21

Dear Family of Creator, Mary felt sufficiently safe
in the embrace of your forgiving and reconciling love
to voice the hope and healing that came from your hospitality.

That was a courageous act of the faith
in the neighborhood where she was singing,
in the region where she gave birth to you.
Roman legions had recently put down resistance and revolt
with a vicious violence that left you and your friends
traumatized by plunder, rape, and butchery.
You heard the cries of Mary and her friends
and acted.
Mary responded with trust and loyalty.

Mary passed that courageous faith on
to her son, you, in Jesus.
After 30 years of being nurtured
in your community of faith in ravaged Nazareth,
you began your public ministry
with a sermon in the synagogue in Nazareth
that echoed your mother's Magnificat.
Your followers remembered the text and the hearers' response.
You preached from the book of the prophet Isaiah.

Here's how Luke recorded that incident
that followed your baptism, your time of testing,
and your early acclaim in the villages of Galilee:

"Jesus came to Nazareth, where he had been brought up.
Entering the synagogue on the Sabbath,
as was his habit,
Jesus stood up to do that reading.
When the book of the prophet Isaiah was handed him,
He unrolled the scroll and found the passage
where it was written:
'The Spirit of our God is upon me:
because the Most High has anointed me
to bring Good News to those who are poor.
God has sent me to proclaim
liberty to those held captive,
recovery of sight to those who are blind,
and release to those in prison—
to proclaim the year of our God's favor.'
Rolling up the scroll, Jesus gave it back to the attendant
and sat down.
The eyes of all in the synagogue were fixed on him.
Then he said to them, 'Today, in your hearing,
this scripture passage is fulfilled.'"[24]

You named the failures of your neighbors
to live out the covenant with Sarah and Abraham
that their heirs were to be a blessing to all the world,
with special care for those whose suffering you had seen.
They were outraged to be called to account in this way.

24. Luke 4:16–21 (IB).

They turned on you with violent intention
but you were enabled to walk away,
leaving the seeds of your message
scattered on the varied soils of your hometown.

You, in turn, have passed that courageous faith onto us.
You have made us ambassadors of your mercy and grace,
of the message of your forgiving and reconciling love.

As ambassadors, we look for alliances.
We seek communities in which you are at work.
We seek to discover the dynamics of your blessing
drawing people into the swing of sanctifying significance.
We listen to their understanding of what's going on
with humble respect.
Then we speak as best we can in that moment
of the kinship that you are creating
and the blessings you invite us to co-compose and play with you.

As Mirian sang a new song, echoing the song of Moses, Mary performs her music through improvisational embodied obedience. Her womb will become the site of the new song of salvation. By her prophetic improvisation on the melody of the song of Israel, Mary sets the stage for her son's enacting of redemption in the flesh for all time.[25]

25. Heltzel, *Resurrection City*, 52.

Prayer 22

Dear Family of Creator, on this Christian day of Sabbath,
as we focus our attention on you and your workings among us,
you have drawn that attention
to how you showed up in the purity cultures of first century Galilee.
It was a society ruled by shoulds, shaming, and shunning.

Purity demanded obedience to the social order of the authorities.
Lack of conformity led to demeaning and dismissing.
Those religious and political authorities lived in a self-righteous fear.
They drew up the rules and regulations,
attributed them to you,
and enforced them with a vengeance.

The imperial system of Jesus' day,
facing a rapid urban concentration of population
and a disruption of the old agrarian economy,
marginalized, impoverished, imprisoned, and killed many people.
In Jesus, you hung out with a lot of them.
You created pockets of inclusion,
you devised ways of sharing resources,
you visited and comforted as you were able in the circumstances.
You cultivated through Jesus
a remembering and a reformulation of your covenant of blessing—

all peoples were to love you, love others, and love themselves.
That was the summation of all your law and prophetic teachings.

I wonder whether you ever danced at parties and clubs?
Did you hang out in that day's equivalents of dance halls?
Were they places where the rejected and the forlorn congregated
to feel some sense of belonging and blessing?
Did those who frequented such gatherings
find in the connections and companionship,
however fleeting,
a sense of sanctifying significance?
Did your presence in Jesus amplify that dignity and worth?
Did people sense something about you being with them
that gave them hope and healing?
I imagine so.

What we know of your public presence
for those three years prior to your crucifixion
indicates that you had developed a deep compassion
for those who suffered the indignities of imperial power.

You nourished hope and healing
among the shunned of that society.

You spoke of and embodied a purity of heart and soul
that was rooted in your forgiving and reconciling love.
You embraced the whole world with its saving influence.

Not even execution for sedition by those authorities
eliminated your presence and influence.
In an act of resurrection that mystifies us still,

you triumphed over death in all its forms
and continued to work among us
with the healing power
that enables all of us, when we choose, to live together
in justice, kindness, and humility.

On this Sabbath, remind us of the potential in that fulfilled promise.

> In Jesus, God did not remove the complexity of the divine life but became a companion for us, inviting us to live freely in the absolute unfathomable depths of grace and divine love. The Son of God's life introduced us to the awesome complexity of the human creature itself. We are much more than we can grasp, understand or certainly control, each of us and all of us together. What I have learned by listening to and watching so many musicians, especially jazz musicians, is what it means to give witness to that complexity. . . . what they have also done in ways quite astounding has been to capture glimpses into the depths of human existence in the presence of God.[26]

26. Jennings, "Seeing God," 14.

Prayer 23

Dear Family of Creator, the origins of jazz lie in the sufferings of slavery,
as you have seen so compassionately
over the generations of the growth and spread
of that musicking community.

The people of Africa who were commodified and commercialized
brought with them to the slave lands
the drumming rhythms of their primal religiosity,
rhythms that resounded with your generative power
and reminded them of their sanctifying significance
in the midst of the traumas of oppression and exploitation.

As they appropriated their own interpretations of Christianity,
they looked to the Exodus story
and its echoes in the Jesus story
to find strength for resilience and resistance.

In the lament traditions of the Bible's songbook, the Psalms,
they found permission to name their traumas bluntly,
to submit their sufferings to you,
and to overcome the power
that their oppressors tried to exercise.

The hymns to freedom that arise from the jazz community
over the generations of that tradition of musicking
are eloquent testimonies to your liberating work among us
for the well-being of your creation.
It is freedom for sanctifying significance
in your flourishing future.
It is the soul of the blues.

These considerations just skim the surface
of the hybridity of your influences
that shaped/shapes the playing of jazz
and its redemptive influence in your world.

Jazz challenged the insecurities and rules
of the dominant white society in North America,
especially in the first sixty years of the twentieth century.
It was denounced as degrading and dangerous.

But the urge to be blessings,
often so deeply felt that no words came to express it,
continued to flow through the community that made this music.

In that urge for dignity and worth,
you were at work nourishing ambassadors of your mercy and grace
to flourish in dance halls and other places
where people gathered to belong and be embraced,
even for a fleeting moment.

This was your latent church,
active in places where people caught glimpses
of your forgiving and reconciling love.

Some connected those glimpses to your manifest church.
Others did not.
But you were at work regardless.

In the midst of this unraveling
of our assumptions about how your church should serve you,
awaken our senses to the lessons you are offering us
in the workings, wit, and wisdom of the jazz community.

Grant us glimpses in these conversations
of the swing of the flourishing future you are generating
and draw us further into it as your partners.

But what does it mean to be a bluesman in the life of the mind? Like my fellow musicians, I've got to forge a unique style and voice that expresses my own quest for truth and love. That means following the quest wherever it leads and bearing whatever cost is required. I must break through isolated academic frameworks while, at the same time, I must build on the best of academic knowledge. I must fuel the fire of my soul so my intellectual blues can set others on fire. And most importantly, I must be a free spirit. I must unapologetically reveal my broken life as a thing of beauty.[27]

27. West, *Brother West*, 5

Prayer 24

Dear Family of Creator, your early church
was drawn into deeper recognition of its common calling
to care for creation with you.

It took time and a dramatic act
to get through to your earliest companions.
Leading up to your execution,
they pretty much abandoned you.
Three years of hanging out with you,
listening to your radical reformulation of your faith for those times,
playing the melodies, harmonies, and rhythms of your gospel
throughout the villages of Galilee,
enjoying the esteem and accolades garnered by your ministry,
and they bailed when the authorities clamped down.

But your patient, pestering presence
did get through to them.
In long talks on the road,
around tables at evening meals,
on beaches over breakfast early in the morning,
in rooms filled with frightened and doubting people,
in another dramatic act with rushing wind and flames of fire,
you played your signature tune
of forgiving and reconciling love

for their inspiration and instruction.
You infused them with the recognition that they were gifted
to bear your blessing into every network they frequented.
In taking up that responsibility with ever deepening consciousness,
they grew into their sanctifying significance.

What they discovered as they matured in their relationship with you
was that you were being true to your declared intention
of breaking down every barrier that divided your beloved humans.
Your Spirit flowed through all peoples at Pentecost,
bringing them to greater awareness and appreciation
of their kinship with each other in you
and their common calling of tending to the welfare of all creation.

We had trouble from the very beginning
in grasping the full redemption offered in this salvation.
It seriously messed with our comforting assumptions.
It posed new possibilities
that would reformulate our ways of living together.
There was sacrifice involved—
of privilege, of power, of prestige,
of property, of presuppositions.

This was a new humanity you were composing,
the one you intended in the first place,
the one we had rebelled against
in our arrogant revolt against partnering with you.

It brought to the attention of our souls
words that you often spoke while in the flesh:
"You have heard it said. . . . , but I say to you . . . ."

What we wanted to hear, and made it so,
was that we were in possession of your wisdom and power
and commanded to make others into our image.
What you were saying
was that we were being enabled and educated
to grow into our responsibilities to embody your image
as a community dancing with delight
in spreading well-being throughout all creation.

What is it in the mess that we have compounded over the generations
that drives your beloved kin to the superficial belonging
that happens in the dance halls of our era—
the dives, the drug dens, the back alleys, the tent cities,
the prisons, the corner bars, the SROs, the porn sites, or the dark web?

It is the trauma of angry violation
inflicted on generation after generation
perpetrated against those whose difference
threatens our superficial security.
We fear losing what is unraveling.
We are too lazy to imagine better alternatives.
We take refuge in self-righteous certainties.
We imprison ourselves
in the fortresses of some purity culture.

You are there with us.
But you are not doing what we expect.
You are undermining the battlements
to free us from our fears.
You are humming with the swing of your salvation.
You are drawing us out of the fortifications

to connect in compassion and companionship
with those we see as threat.
You are forging a new humanity
inspired and instructed by the fruits of your Spirit—
love, joy, peace, patience, kindness, generosity,
faithfulness, and gentleness.
You are partnering with us to compose ourselves
into a peace corps of ambassadors of those attitudes
and behaviors.
Like your first ambassadors,
it is taking us a while to get it.

In the places we are looking for the redemption
of hospitality, hope, and healing,
you are giving us little bites of your feast for flourishing.
You are stimulating our sense of significance to get our attention
and awaken us to the fact that there is so much more
than we ever hoped for or imagined
when we came looking for our dignity and worth
in a dance or two, or a drink or two, or a dime bag or two.

But you come looking for us in those places.
You make them sacred space for meeting us
with your forgiving and reconciling love,
so desperately needed among us
if we are to change the course of our future.

Tune all of our senses to appreciate your work of redemption
and ally with it
in all of the communities with whom you invite us to hang out.

[In a new jazz age] hope, option, new possibility open up. Those in power see that it's not their power the church wants, but to do *mishpat*, to love *hesed*, and to walk humbly with God.

The church then opposes, not by pushing back face-to-face, but by improvising, creating new options, looking at a third way, one without an oppressive hierarchy. This is creation, thinking outside the box, finding hope, attending to love, playing jazz in the beloved city. . . .

As jazz musicians improvise together to make music, so, too, should prophetic Christians improvise for justice today. Through improvisation, jazz players are able to make new music in new places—together. Embracing a jazz consciousness, it is time for Christians to gather up the theatre of the oppressed, imagining and improvising love and justice in the city, amongst the powers and principalities. In doing this, we lay foundations with rejected stones; we garden where no growth could happen, where rivers flow freely in dry, paved places.[28]

28. Heltzel, *Resurrection City*, 169–70.

Prayer 25

Dear Family of Creator, the disciplines
of staying in partnership with you
are embedded in the life of your corps of ambassadors,
your church.
That is where you have found me and formed me
through transformation after transformation,
one conversation after another,
one improvisation after another.

The current corps with which you have embedded me
is Brentwood Presbyterian Church in Burnaby, BC.
We are a lively, diverse, and curious
community of your friends.
We strive to nourish souls to flourish in your mercy and grace
through welcoming, worshiping, learning and serving.
We've composed our own declaration of our faith in you
that we say together on Sunday mornings.
This statement of faith is in the form of the story
you are inviting us join
as we mature into our sanctifying significance.

"In the beginning, God created the heavens and the earth
and declared them to be very good.

God then created humanity, in all our diversity,
to cultivate blessing throughout the world.

Rejecting the limits of their power,
our ancestors rebelled against God's vision of goodness.
By continuing to rebel against God's constraints,
We compound the pain of toil, tyranny, trauma, and death.

But God never gave up on us, as the Spirit reveals in the Scriptures.

In a definitive act of reconciling forgiveness,
God became incarnate among us.
In the life, death, resurrection, and ascension of Jesus of Nazareth,
God restored the original goodness of creation
as a commonwealth enjoyed on earth as it is in heaven.
The Holy Spirit continues to work out the fulfilment of that act.

Through the church universal in which we participate,
the Holy Spirit nourishes us to flourish as God's friends
through welcoming, worshiping, learning, and serving.
By God's grace, in Jesus Christ, through the Holy Spirit,
we know what it is to be loved and to love
amidst all the problems of the world,
and we are equipped, empowered, and sent
to sow the seeds of God's peace in all our circles of influence.

In the end, God's love
will transform the heavens and the earth,
and bring justice, peace, and joy
to every dimension of creation."[29]

29. *Brentwood Declaration*, https://www.brentwoodpcc.com/brentwood-declaration.

You cultivate our alliance with you
through welcoming, worshiping, learning, and serving.

In our dizzying diversity,
we play complex improvisations on this love story.
We shame and shun each other far too easily
because of our differences.

That's a traumatic and tragic part of our ongoing rebellion.

In your patient persistence, heal us of this warring madness.
Bring us into sync with your musicking for our mutual delight.
Fill us with the rhythms of grace and gratitude.
Keep us focused on the melody of forgiving and reconciling.
Inspire us with the harmonies you are composing for us all.

Morning prayers like these,
in the intimacy of your devotion to me,
proceed from and are sustained by
the community that is you and your people
throughout the world.
They are drawn together by you in churches and in dance halls,
in affluent enclaves and impoverished slums,
in gatherings where your presence is recognized
and in those where it is not.

You are omnipresent in your world.
You invite us to discern your presence
and draw attention to it with a bold humility
that keeps your teachable spirit flourishing in all our networks.

There is a chord chart
from which you are encouraging us to play
in this jazz ensemble that is your church:

Love you. Love others. Love yourselves.

Make that melody the earworm of our lives.
In every encounter you have with us,
hone our ability to play it with great delight.

I often wonder what it would be like if we composed a jazz-shaped Christianity.

What if there was a way for Christians to live with the tensions of our faith and to embrace their beauty?

What if you and I experienced church like a jazz ensemble (listening to the beat of the image of God in each of us) and community meant that you and I felt connected, not only to those we can see, but also with those who have followed (in past generations) and have yet (in future generations) to follow Jesus?

What if there is another way to know the Scriptures? What if we experienced the word of God as a song that sets us free to compose, a melody that has room for our voice to join in with the ancients?

What if every moment of life with Jesus is pregnant with promise, containing the potential to be a one-of-a-kind masterpiece?

What if so much that has gone wrong with America has also produced something that is right and good, allowing for us to live and love with soul because we understand why caged birds sing?

What if we could find the groove and in the process live in IT?

These are the questions I have been asking in the hope of composing a jazz-shaped faith that will lead me closer to the kingdom of God in our midst.[30]

30. Gelinas, *Finding*, 15–16.

Prayer 26

Dear Family of Creator, what, then,
have you revealed to us about your divine call to dance with you?

You have modeled for us in your incarnation in Jesus of Nazareth
a way of being human with you and others in your creation
that is rooted in your forgiving and reconciling love
for the whole world.

You have assured us that we are beloved partners with you,
in spite of our ongoing fears and failures,
in the family business of caring for creation
within the networks to which you send us
as ambassadors of your mercy and grace.

You have demonstrated your patience and persistence
in transforming us into the dancers you created us to be.
You are drawing us
from an aimless wandering into a focused wondering,
from the dread of darkness into your illuminating light,
from debilitating loneliness into enabling community,
from crushing confusion into exhilarating clarity,
from depressing despair to elated joy,
and from the fear of death into faith in eternal life.

You have sown into the imaginings of our souls
the insight that you already are acting redemptively
in the workings, wisdom, and wit of jazz.
You are inviting us to see in that form of musicking
new ways of understanding the church's missioning
through which you are nourishing our sanctifying significance.
You have inspired us with the prophetic vision
composed so eloquently in Mary's improvisation on Hannah's song
as they contemplated the birthing of your ambassadors,
Samuel and Jesus.
That vision was centred on justice, kindness,
and a humble companionship with you
in friendship and faithfulness.
Samuel spoke your purpose to a traumatized world
filled with stress injuries of all kinds.
You did the same in Jesus.

But how will we respond to your call?
What dance steps will you teach us in that responsiveness?
What responsibilities will generate our sanctifying significance?

This word "inspiration" is fundamental. It means being "in-spirited" by something else, something more. It means one has gotten out of the way and let a greater force or power take hold—perhaps the music, perhaps the muses, perhaps God. Coltrane believed it was God, and gave constant thanks for it as something given and not his own. Regardless of how one names it, this gift empowers the state of self-transcendence so often extolled by mystics and artists alike. And it is a gift, something that "comes" and indwells like the spirit at Pentecost. Such a gift cannot be possessed or conjured mechanically and on command. Paradoxically, it comes as the artist lets go and steps forward into the open, willing to re-enter the world differently, loosening his or her grip on reality as it is or may seem to be. This brings us 'round full circle to the dynamic quality of jazz, for openness charges the moment with possibility, the potential for creative vitality and novelty. . . . there is much at stake for all of us. Perhaps the spiritual life is like a jazz performance. It may lead us to think differently about faith, tradition, cultural differences, church, and God's work in our midst.[31]

31. Reynolds, "JAZZ," 37–38.

Second Movement

Considering Humanity's Response

Prayer 27

Dear Family of Creator, jazz is an art form
composed around a dynamic of call and response,
summons and significance.
If we are all jazz musicians
by virtue of living together through conversations,
what are the most appropriate responses we can imagine
to your embrace of all humanity in Jesus Christ?

You summon us to the freedom
that friendship and collaboration with you can bring.
You summon us out of our rebellion into our responsibility.
You summon us to be the blessings
you intended us to be.

In Jesus Christ,
in ways we understand only in part,
you liberated us from our rebellious selves
to become partners with you
in cultivating flourishing throughout all the networks
in which you have embedded us.

It's a bit like the gig life of a jazz musician.
You find places where it would be good for us to play.
Every act of playing our sacred suites

is enabled by an ecosystem of supporters.
There are those who build and maintain the venue.
There are those who offer hospitality every time we play.
There are those who attend the events,
fans, friends, and strangers who might just become fans and friends.
There are those who write and arrange the music.
There are those of who play the music at that event.
There are those who clean up after us.
Through all of these people,
however awakened to it or not they may be at that event,
you are at work generating hospitality, hope, and healing.
In each experience of belonging and blessing,
of sanctifying significance,
you nourish our freedom to flourish as your ambassadors
of your forgiving and reconciling love.

Oscar Peterson wrote his "Hymn to Freedom" in 1962,
recorded it late that year
and released in 1963 on his *Night Train* album,
dedicated to his father who worked as a porter on the trains.
Harriette Hamilton wrote the lyrics a little later.

"When every heart joins every heart
and together yearns for liberty,
that's when we'll be free.

When every hand joins every hand
and together moulds our destiny,
that's when we'll be free.

Any hour, any day, the time soon will come
when we will live in dignity,
that's when we'll be free.

When everyone joins in our song
and together sings in harmony,
that's when we'll be free."

"All the lyrics had to do," wrote Hamilton,
"was to express in very simply language
the hope for unity, peace and dignify for mankind [sic].
It was easy to write."[32]

These are words
that capture the simplicity on the other side of complexity.
They lay out the notes of the chord
around which you are calling us to improvise
as we respond to your summons
to partner with you in the care of all creation,
heart joined to heart in longing for liberty,
hand joined to hand in working for a dignified destiny,
everyone joining with their harmonies in your hymn to freedom.

The responses appropriate to the gift of this kind of freedom,
this gift of liberation that you have been cultivating
generation after generation,
demand our souls, our lives, our all.
That kind of "all in" playing
characterizes the best of jazz
and the best of church.

32. Canadian Songwriters Hall of Fame, "Hymn to Freedom."

Jurgen Moltmann explored the dynamics of freedom
throughout his reflections on his experiences of you
as the source of hope in community for the flourishing of your creation.
In *The Spirit of Life*, here's how he put it:

"To what is freedom's hope directed?
'How much more,' Paul often says,
when he thinking about 'freedom from. . . .'
but is talking about 'freedom for. . . .'
How much greater is the future than the past!
How much greater is God's grace than the sins of men and women!
How much more is freedom in its own world
than mere liberation from slavery!
It is true that in the history we experience
it is easier to name the negative thing from which we want to be freed
than the positive thing for which we hope to be free.
But it is hope for the greater future
which leads us to ever new experiences in history.
That is the surplus of hope in life,
and the added value of the future in history."[33]

You summon us into a freedom for your future
with the assurance that you will be with us always
as we improvise in the composing
of your commonweal of justice and peace.

Let's explore the dynamics of such freedom
for playing your mercy and grace like a jazz group with you
one conversation after another
in the next several prayers.

33. Moltmann, *Spirit*, 68.

Improvising isn't winging it. Which is why, in mastering the craft of improvisation, jazz musicians have learned to do things that the inhabitants of other collective undertakings merely dream about being able to do, namely:

- creating a culture that fosters innovation;
- taking uncertainty as an opportunity rather than a threat;
- encouraging risk-taking while seeing mistakes as learning opportunities;
- fostering an openness to voices with something new to say;
- seeing diversity as a source of creativity by developing multiple perspectives on complex problems.

If you're imagining that in pulling this off, jazz musicians have a unique perspective on the nature of leadership, you'd be right.[34]

34. Hayman, *Tale*, 155.

Prayer 28

Dear Family of Creator, ten freedoms come to mind
that arise from your nurturing of your image in us
as we mature into our responsibilities
as members of your body,
your church, your corps of ambassadors,
both visible and invisible, manifest and latent.

In "the vast river of jazz"—imagine the Mississippi—
these freedoms have given people resilience
through unspeakable pain and suffering
as well as found elated expression
in songs of joy that healed the soul.

Each freedom is interdependent with all the others.
Together, they compose a suite of sanctifying significance
that draws us into the flow of your redeeming mercy and grace
as contributors to your care of your creation.

Your first freedom is the freedom to hang out
with all of your beloved creatures.
This is your gift of belonging in your family
and contributing to your family business.
These are the people and their habitats
within which you enliven our sanctifying significance.

You liberate us from our fears
of being rejected and ostracized.

Your second freedom is
the freedom to listen for your providential activity
throughout all of creation.
It is your gift of being with us always.
You sustain us and transform us
as you encounter us in opportunities to bless.
You liberate us from a fearful withdrawal
into the silent labyrinths of our loneliness.

Your third freedom is
the freedom to imagine what we can contribute
to the possibilities you are provoking us into.
It is your gift of partnership.
You generate opportunities for us to add our unique capabilities
to those of others in our networks of inspiration and influence
to harmonize our endeavors with your mercy and grace.
You liberate us from a sense of worthlessness
that blocks our access to your life-giving nutrients.

Your fourth freedom is
the freedom to engage in dialogues
with your delightfully diverse networks of creatures
in our common home about our common well-being.
It is your gift of discernment.
You continually challenge us with new perspectives and possibilities
as we explore our passions and problems with others.
Liberate us from a lazy reluctance
to converse with those who differ from us.

Your fifth freedom is
the freedom to unlearn and relearn
how to get the mix of attitudes and behaviors right
as we seek to be faithful, wise, and effective in our contexts.
It is your gift of education by failure and success.
You stay with us when we misunderstand
and support us when we recognize
your workings in your world.
Liberate us from our misrepresentations of you
by the continual illumination of your Spirit.

Your sixth freedom is
the freedom to rely on others with trust and respect.
It is your gift of collaboration.
You amplify the benefits of our efforts
as you arrange them into effective blessings
for all that come into our spheres of influence.
Liberate us from our self-righteous compulsions
to be independent and dominant.

Your seventh freedom is
the freedom to respect the tradition for its insights
and find ways to reformulate it,
to improve the reverberations of our ways of living together
on the complex ecosystem of your creation.
It is your gift of traditioned innovation.
You never stop reminding us that we are all interdependent
in the complex matrix of systems
that sustain and enhance life in your world.
Liberate us from the arrogant assumption
that we know how to control them for the common good.

Your eighth freedom is
the freedom to organize our collaborations
with just enough structure to enable us to work creatively together.
It is your gift of sacred coordination.
By inspiring us with a common vision of SHALOM,
you foster the blending of our talents
to spread your mercy and grace far and wide.
Liberate us from the restricted visions
that deprive your beloved creatures and their homes
of their rights to be blessings.

Your nineth freedom
is the freedom to disrupt patterns of thinking and acting
that raise barriers to your work of redemption
for the whole of your creation.
It is the gift of challenging the process.
You summon us to see things differently
so that we can mature in our partnership with you
in nourishing all your desires to flourish for our mutual delight.
Liberate us from the lazy comfort
that accepts things as they are
as the way they are supposed to be.

Your tenth freedom is
the freedom to delight in the surprising ways
you will draw us into the dance of your delight
at the flourishing of your creation.
It is your gift of joy.
You keep us open to change to ally more fully with you
as you encourage and equip us
to be responsible citizens of your flourishing future.

This is revealed so clearly every Easter morning
when you enable us to join you in the dance
and promise to live in us as we live in you.
Liberate us from the deadening despair
that infects us when we lose touch with you.

Take us deeper into these freedoms for flourishing
that you have sown in the depths of our souls.

Illumine these benefits in the prayers that follow.

Make of these prayers a suite of suggestions
indicating how we might play the lives you have gifted us.

Alert us to the richness and complexities
of the interdependencies that sustain and enhance our lives.
Open up redemptive possibilities
for co-composing an embracing kinship
among all your creatures and their habitats.

Awaken us to the sanctifying significance you offer
and the responsibilities for blessing
we find ourselves offered and accepting
as you encounter us in all the networks
into which you send us.

In all of this self-composure in companionship with you,
lead us all over the dance floor
in your swing of grace and gratitude.

It was in part from African sources that the vast river of jazz emerged. Michael O'Stadhail writes of jazz improvisation:

> Moody solos. Unique. The stamp of one voice;
> Then pure concert as an ensemble improvises,
> Hearing in each other harmonies of cross-purpose,
> As though being ourselves we're more capacious.

. . . Freedom is not first of all chosen by us, but it is mediated through others, as they give themselves to us and us to them, and never more so than in the community God has provided for just this to happen. In this God-given ensemble, we find we are able to accommodate others we have previously shunned. To be drawn into the hospitable singing of a church can be a powerful enacted metaphor of just this. A complex sound comes to us and envelops us. We do not choose this note or that to be "with"; we are, so to speak, baptized into its notes-in-relation, and through this sound, into a body of flesh-and-blood people. We are not smothered, but we can find our own voice as we are released to listen to and harmonize with others: "being ourselves we're more capacious."[35]

35. Begbie, *Resounding*, 290–291.

Prayer 29

Dear Family of Creation, your first freedom,
is the freedom to hang out
with all of your beloved creatures.
This is your gift of belonging in your family
and contributing to your family business.

In a culture so often focused on "freedom from"
restrictions of any kind,
it is often hard to appreciate the importance of belonging.

Until, of course, we lose that sense of affinity and inclusion.

Then our sense of isolation and loneliness imprisons us.
Our resilience and resolve weaken.
A lethargy descends and shrouds us.
Feeling cut off and cutting ourselves off further
becomes a vicious pattern of self-decomposition.

There are lots of people connecting with us
in lots of callous ways.
They want to exploit us for their own advantage,
however they may define that.
They offer "miracle" cures for our discomforts and dissatisfactions.
"Consume this!" and "Consume that!"

We let them numb the pain with their cures.
We let them enslave us with their promises.

We settle for mere material survival
in subtle (or not so subtle) forms of slavery.

Connection alone, however attached we become to its promises,
does not generate the freedom for which you have created us.

Your freedom is a welcome
into a community of courageous compassion
beyond our wildest and fondest imaginings.
It is a gift of positive intimacy
that heals us into a hope
that is shaped, sustained, and enriched
by your forgiving and reconciling love
with every breath we take.

Every breath is an opportunity
to accept your liberation from our past
and choose life in community over death in isolation.
Every breath is a gift that makes that possible.

There is an intriguing calm
in the feeling evoked by the words "hanging out."
It's not something overly planned or structured.
It's not something overburdened with agendas.
It's not something fraught with dangers.
It's just—"hanging out."

It is a space for comraderies,
for play and creativity,
for cultivating the sanctifying significance
of every person participating and contributing.

It is a space where you can open up
new opportunities for the flourishing
in the networks we frequent.
This is not a space for monological messaging
but of dialogical discernment.

The substance of the conversations you provoke in this space
are not rigidly pre-programmed.
A specific topic or melody line may get them started
but you blow where you will as the playing proceeds.
The conversations cover
the whole range of what it means to be human—
the pains, the joys, the sacrifices, the achievements,
how to be a good citizen of the earth,
how to play your part with others
in the redemption of the creation.

Awaken us ever more consciously to your presence in our hanging out.

Jazz is crowdsourcing. Jazz shares. It trades. In the marketplace of what gets played and remembered, jazz also votes. We can argue all we want about the social utility of jazz—I happen to think it's high—but as an art form and mode of education, jazz is certainly learning by acting, by doing, by social exchange. With jazz, you master notes and chords, how to blow into a horn instrument and coax sound from strings or a drumhead or what you have. But you also learn how to be and do and live. You say yes to the mess by surrendering control—by opening yourself up to the capriciousness of the crowd, with no guarantee of success for your efforts. Ultimately, that takes one quality above all others: courage.[36]

36. Barrett, *Yes*, 117.

Prayer 30

Dear Family of Creator, your second freedom
is to listen for your activities
in all the hanging out that we do.
It's tuning our ears to the sounds of your salvation
at work in the complex interdependencies
that shape our lives in your world.

You work through everything that you created.
You reveal that in provocative ways in musicking,
ways that resonate in realms of our consciousness
that are not always accessed easily by words alone.

The listening that you invite us into
is collective, collegial, communal, and creative.
It is done in community, for community,
by the community of the whole of your creation.
It is multi-faceted, with voices coming from many sources.
It is polyvocal in calling
for the changes you want to see made
in the ways we live together on your earth.

When we open ourselves to the wisdom of such listening,
we are liberated from the reductionist confines
of seeing the world from only one perspective.

We can honor what we have come to know already,
but be open to new ways of understanding
your faith in us and ours in you.

In the midst of our dialogues with each other,
in ways that honor, but are not controlled by,
all the views expressed,
you stimulate and calm our ways of seeing your flourishing future
that guide us into our next experiments
in generating the harmonies of mercy and grace
that you are provoking.

Liberate us from the prisons we build out of our fears.
Release us from the lethargies that hinder us
from exploring new insights and possibilities.
Shatter the shells of our self-righteousness
to let your light illumine the darknesses
of our limiting assumptions.

Draw us close into your dance of love.
Guide our basic steps.
Encourage us to try variations
that add to the delightful flow of your flourishing.
Embrace us into the joy of your kinship
in caring for your creation.

Churches could learn much from reflecting on a jazz band. Here are a group of people who work very hard at listening, yet give up nothing of themselves in the process, but in fact only gain a true sense of themselves in the common task of making music, producing sound that makes a central statement that exists only through the constitutive performances of each musician. [It is] the many driving toward the one—the one sound, and the one ecstasy of playing well. . . .

Musicians live and play in tight quarters, which is not only a matter of the given but also a matter of choice. They need closeness to hear. Would that Christians could grasp this truth of our witness. We don't simply need each other, we need to be close together in order to truly hear the words we should be saying to the world and, equally important, to hear more clearly the voice of the world, in its pain, suffering, and longing.[37]

37. Jennings, "Seeing God," 15.

Prayer 31

Dear Family of Creator, your third freedom
is the freedom to contribute to the care of your creation.
We have been given capabilities no other creature enjoys.
We've misused them with a gross irresponsibility
that has compounded over generations.
It has become embedded in our systems of living together.
It drags us into labyrinths of loss and loathing
that imprison us in lethargy.

We conquer or cringe rather than contribute.

But your image within us has not died,
however dead it may seem.
You have never given up on the potential of your human creatures.
You have never stopped pursuing us
with your invitation to rejoin the rejoicing
in the dance hall of your creation.

You summon us back into being dance partners.
You awaken us to the rhythms pulsating in your creating,
the melodies playing in your forgiving and reconciling,
and the harmonies being made of our responding.

This is the freedom we see in the prison cells
of the people who recount your saving actions down through the ages.
Those of us who you have awakened
to our human dignity and worth,
being created in your image,
cannot allow souls to be imprisoned.

We walk with you, in you,
wherever we may be.

Our freedom to contribute to the care of your creation
rests secure in your life-giving companionship
that nothing in life or death can kill.
Neither trouble, calamity, persecution, hunger, nakedness,
danger, nor violence,
neither the present, nor the future, nor anything else in all creation,
can separate us from your steadfast love.

You created us with a life-giving sanctifying significance.
Nothing we can devise or concoct
in the farthest reaches of our rebellions
can eliminate that sense of who we are.
That hunch, that inkling, that intuition
is constantly at work among us and within us,
inspiring us to come to ourselves as partners with you.

In that partnership, we find our true freedom
for collaborating with you
in contributing to your justice with kindness and humility.

In the prisons of our own fears and loathings,
we denigrate ourselves with memories of failures.
We focus on imperfections and impurities.
We buy into the standards of those who are oppressing us.
We accept their belittling and make it our own.
We are traumatized into terrified subservience.

But you never leave us abandoned
in such demeaning loneliness.
Your riffs of mercy and grace witnessing to our dignity and worth
keep resonating in our souls,
waiting for us to hear them.

Marianne Williamson, in a quote often mistakenly attributed
to Nelson Mandela,
captures eloquently the resonance of this companionship.

"Our deepest fear is not that we are inadequate.
Our deepest fear is that we are powerful beyond measure.
It is our light, not our darkness, that most frightens us.
We ask ourselves, 'Who am I
to be brilliant, gorgeous, talented, fabulous?'
Actually, who are you not to be?
You are a child of God.
Your playing small doesn't serve the world.
There's nothing enlightened about shrinking
so that other people won't feel insecure around you.
We are all meant to shine, as children do.
As we're liberated from our own fear,
our presence automatically liberates others."[38]

38. Williamson, *Return*, 165.

Too many within your churches today
have bought into the delusion of total depravity
and misrepresented you as an angry God
who binds us with rigid beliefs and rules
in order to win your favor.
They have lost the knowledge of your sacred paradox
that we are treasures in earthen vessels.
Instead, they spend their precious energies
seeking escape from your imagined wrath
by demanding conformity.

That's the kind of rigid religiosity you challenged directly
in your teachings as Jesus of Nazareth.
You invited creative, improvised contributions
to the melody of Jesus' summary of your intent for us—
love you, love others, and love ourselves.

Use these prayers and the considerations they provoke
to awaken your human creatures
to our capabilities to ally with you in saving your world.

Jazz musicians tend to practice a humble boldness when it comes to their craft. They know that they are vessels of something much larger than they are. They know that there is a gift element about preparing to play, and playing. They know that it is not just about human intention; it is about the movement of the muse, the Spirit. But this knowledge of human limitation does not keep them from stretching long and wide into the experience of creating. They, more often than not, dive into the mystery and dare to play with the mystery. Jazz artists lean into creativity. They accept the call to create at face value. They don't question their right to be cocreators with God. They embrace and live out of a deliberate, creative disposition.[39]

39. Jones, *Jazz of Preaching*, 66.

Prayer 32

Dear Family of Creation, your fourth freedom
is the freedom to engage in dialogues
with your delightfully diverse networks of creatures
in our common home about our common well-being.
It is your gift of discernment through conversing
about the most puzzling paradox of human life—
great pain co-mingling with great joy.

We live through conversing.

With every breath of your grace we inhale,
you oxygenate our beings for meaningful conversations
with others who are contributing
to the realization of your flourishing future.

With every breath of your grace we inhale,
our souls are ignited to integrate the wisdom
you are composing
through our intuitions, emotions, and reasonings
into faithful, wise, and effective responses
that enhance the influence of your forgiving and reconciling.

With every breath of your grace we inhale,
you shape our destiny as valued members of your body on earth,
doing your work for your world.

With every breath of gratitude we exhale,
you give us the opportunity to shape sounds
that show calm, curiosity, and appreciation.

With every breath of gratitude we exhale,
you offer us the courage to manage our fears,
the imagination to explore possibilities,
and the self-esteem to be authentic.

With every breath of gratitude we exhale,
you send our sanctifying significance into your world
with the potential for enhancing the well-being
of all who are touched by it.

We co-compose whatever we are doing through conversations,
one after another.
Conversations with you, with others, and with ourselves—
in dialogue that digs deep into your will,
respecting the voices of all involved—
are hotbeds of positive innovation.
They are the matrix within which transformation happens.
They are the forge where your future is fashioned.

Of primal importance in this dynamic,
as we consider what the church might learn from jazz,
is the connection between conversation and music.

In an improvisation on this insight, Stephen Nachmanovich
recognizes conversation as our most common form of jazz.

Nachmanovich is a violinist, music educator, and composer. He wrote:

"We are all improvisers.
The most common form of improvisation
is ordinary speech.
As we talk and listen,
we are drawing on a set of building blocks (vocabulary)
and rules for combining them (grammar).
They have been given to us by our culture.
But the sentences we make with them
may never have been said before
and may never be said again.
Every conversation is a form of jazz.
The act of instantaneous creation
is as ordinary to us as breathing."[40]

For too long, your church has deluded itself
that it understands your revelation sufficiently
to be the authoritative narrator of your story of salvation.
It's been imprisoned in its monological messaging,
taking as its norm the imperial formulations of the faith
flowing from the takeover of the church by the Roman empire.
It's used a tightly-scripted symphony score
to enforce right thinking and right acting.

As those imperial pretensions
reached their zenith and began to unravel

40. Nachmanovich, *Free Play*, 17.

over the past 500 years,
your church floundered in its failures and fears.
You kept speaking to us through your prophets,
but we were far too often deafened by our fearful arrogance.

One of those prophetic streams of voices came from jazz.
In itself, it is a delightfully diverse network
of oppressed and pained people,
remembering the rhythms of dignity from their African origins,
resilient in the pain of their oppression,
and resonant with their hopes of a providential freedom
to contribute their gifts to your work in your world.

They do this by listening to the voices of that community today,
drawing with respect on the traditions of their ancestors,
but contributing with courage to new expressions
that nourish the liberating values that have inspired them.

Remind us anew every morning
that every conversation matters.
Forgive us the conversations that hurt and divide.
Redeem us in the conversations that forgive and reconcile.
Assure us that with every breath we take,
you are generating an opportunity to be a blessing.

I want dialogue. The quality of community in ensemble is central to everything I've done. Jazz is an in-the-moment narrative, and it's different every time. No other music in the Western world is like that.[41]

41. Hayman, *Tale*, 82.

Prayer 33

Dear Family of Creator, your fifth freedom
is the freedom to unlearn and relearn.
It is the freedom for being converted, for being redeemed.
It is the freedom to grow into wisdom and stature—
into your image in us.

How that happens—
the social networks and interdependencies that facilitate it,
the inspirations and influences that you exercise through them—
are all illuminated in the life of Jesus of Nazareth, your Christ.
The conversations that formed your presence with us
in that time and place
revealed enough about your intentions
for us to partner with you in playing the world's salvation.

Jesus learned the traditions of his ancestors so well
that he found the treasures of your composing
in the midst of the earthenness of the ancestral vessels.
Running through the complicated and conflicted history
of his people and their responsibilities in your world,
he discerned the arc of your goodness in the blessings generated.
He then played on the patterns of your grace and gratitude
in ways with which his kin and neighbors could resonate,

drawing them into the swing of sanctifying significance
in a world that denigrated their dignity and worth.

Innovation, for Jesus, arose from between the lines of the tradition.
Your refiner's fire burned bright in Jesus.
His learning, unlearning, and relearning
arose from the freedom you gave yourself in him to reform.
You proposed and modeled ways of composing our living together
that nourished love, joy, peace, patience, kindness, generosity,
faithfulness, and gentleness.
These are the dance steps you are teaching us in your dance halls.

There is much to unlearn
in our mechanical, industrial, technocratic, digital culture
of oppressive manipulations.
The many are controlled by the few.
The few have developed systems they don't understand.
The planet and its inhabitants have been forced
to learn, to adapt, and to comply.

The limits of this materialistic growth are more and more evident.
But calls for unlearning and relearning get lost in the din
of stubborn assumptions and strident assurances
that we're on the right track.

This is the kind of freedom to reformulate
our patterns of playing together in the dance halls of our lives
that we find in the workings, wisdom, and wit of jazz.
There is a profound sense of belonging to a life-giving tradition.
There is an urge to learn and understand it more deeply.
There is an attraction to contribute constructively

to its continuation and expansion.
There is a realization that to do that in new contexts,
improvisations and new compositions must be tried.
If these contributions fail to better the blessings generated,
they are refined or replaced.

You partner with us in working out the welfare of your world
by inspiring and instructing us constantly to relearn new ways
of doing justice with kindness and humility
through the resonant illumination of your Holy Spirit.

These journeys through the dynamics of unlearning and relearning
take a courage to live into your freedom
that comes only in relationship with you.
That relationship, by your mercy and grace, is always there.
Our consciousness of it is very much a work in progress.

Your patience with us as we move
into and out of misunderstandings of you
is a wonderful gift.

Awaken us to your provocations to love and good works
as we compose our lives together, one conversation after another.

It all goes from imitation to assimilation to innovation. You move from the imitation stage to the assimilation stage when you take little bits of things from different people and weld them into an identifiable style—creating your own style. Once you've created your own sound and you have a good sense of the history of the music, then you think of where the music hasn't gone and where it can go—and that's innovation.[42]

42. Berliner, *Thinking*, 120.

Prayer 34

Dear Family of Creator, your sixth freedom
is the freedom to rely on others with trust and respect.
It is your gift of collaboration.
You amplify the benefits of our endeavors
as you arrange them into effective blessings
for all who come into our networks of cooperation.

We have been shaped in so many ways
by a culture that idolizes "freedom from" such attachments,
especially in the great New-World experiments in the Americas.
We are bombarded by orders to be "free to be me,"
with "me" usually involving buying this product or that service.

Your invitation is, be "free to be we."
You have made us for companionship
with you, with others, with your creation,
and with our best selves in those relationships.
The authenticity that resonates most deeply in us
is a friendship rooted in trust and loyalty
that mirrors your faith in us as your partners.

Some of your ambassadors,
entrusted with the service of making sense of your workings,
have suggested that Christian freedom

is a matter of changing “masters,”
of moving from slavery to this master or that master
to slavery to you.

But is “master” really the best designation for you?

What do we do with your assurance
that we are no longer slaves but friends?

What does “obedience” and “submission” feel like
in such a friendship?

To mature into this unique enlivening relationship,
we accept your invitation
to ally with you in mutual trust and respect.

It’s a unique decision.
It arises from our deep need to belong,
to be in a nourishing companionship,
to find sufficient safety in a relationship
to open ourselves to learning how to live freely,
beyond the confines of our fearfulness,
into the courage that comes from our friendship with you.

You awaken us more and more to your true intention
of making us representatives of the fruits of your salvation
that are being revealed to us in our friendship—
love, joy, peace, patience, kindness, generosity,
faithfulness, and gentleness.
This kind of alignment with your vision
provokes us to the unique freedom that is friendship with you.

You listen to our concerns
with an ear for our aspirations.

You empathize with our struggles
with a heart for our capabilities.

You appreciate our potential
with a commitment to encourage our initiative.

You dynamize our contributions
to provoke sanctifying significance.

Your merciful and gracious energy
leads us to ally with you
in integrating our rich diversity
into a swinging fellowship of friends
playing our deepest sorrows and joys
in the groove of your forgiveness and reconciliation.

As jazz musicians know from the roots of their tradition,
the allying with you that is jazz finds its voice
when you hear our cries of anguish in abandonment.
You see our suffering.
You hear our laments.
You feel our pain.
And you embrace us in friendship.
You create a safe enough space
for us to realize we can do something about the pain.

Maybe it's "just" to sing the blues.
But it's singing.

It's our response to your call to worthiness.
It's honest in its rawness
and hopeful in its resilience.
That's life-giving for all who can hear.

In this kind of friendship,
you liberate us from the confines
of our denigrating and divisive conventions.
It is a new freedom from tired formulations of our faith
that have misrepresented your forgiving and reconciling love
incarnate in Jesus of Nazareth.
It is freedom from obedience to dictates and demands.
It is freedom from submission to shame and shoulds.
It's freedom from the cultural pressures
to be independent and dominant.

You invite us into improvisational experiments
in composing better ways of living together
in the rhythms and harmonies of the chord chart
of justice, peace, and joy.
In these endeavors to improve our caring for creation,
you summon forth all of the gifts you have given to us
communally and personally.
You lead us into your flourishing future one conversation after another,
always alert to the possibilities
for greater justice, kindness, and humility
and always honing our capabilities for contributing.

Lead on, O Master of Swing!

Trio (three in one) playing at best is a situation in which the participants willingly support each other, working together as one and going along with the "driver's" directions, each player bringing virtuosity, optimism, mutual respect, good will, and, of course, the desire to "make it feel good" for all human beings in the general proximity. Three great players together do not necessarily make a good team. There should be that intangible ideal "to take flight." The marvellous gift of increased camaraderie comes about from this shared ideal. I have always believed that in addition to the music itself, it was the special relationship among the players that the listener was hearing and sensing.[43]

43. Alexander, *Impressions*, 1

Prayer 35

Dear Family of Creator, your seventh freedom
is the freedom to respect the tradition for its insights
and to find ways to reformulate them
to improve the reverberations of your intention
on our ways of living together now
in the complex and ever-changing dynamics
of the ecosystem of your creation.

It is your gift of "traditioned innovation."
I came across that phrase in the work of L. Gregory Jones,
once Dean of Duke Divinity School
and now President of Belmont University.[44]

You remind us that we are all interdependent
in the complex matrix of systems
that sustain and enhance life in your world.

Traditioned innovation is your way
of assuring that your communion of saints,
our ancestors in your relationships with us
down through the generations,
are still part of the conversations
through which we co-create your flourishing future.

44. Jones and Hogue, *Navigating*, xviii.

We imitate their riffs and phrases to communicate.
We assimilate their wisdom as we discern through dialogue.
We innovate in empathy
as we sense the pain out of which and into which
we are playing your tunes of redeeming mercy and grace.

You have entrusted to us untold numbers of words
through which the stories of your love for your creation
got handed down from generation to generation.

You have entrusted to us countless songs and scores
that take us to depths of companionship
those words alone cannot reach.

As we gather these gifts together
into the musicking that goes on in your dance halls,
draw our attention to the dominant chords
that convey your intention
for our contributions to our communities today.
Make them constant refrains in our networks of nourishing.
Keep them in tune with your purpose.
Take this "stuck song syndrome"
and use it to enhance our sanctifying significance.

In that process, grant us the courage
to innovate with faithfulness, wisdom, and effectiveness
in our missioning with you in the care of your creation.

Faithfulness in your traditioning of us in your service
involves focusing on your intentions
as revealed in your incarnation in Jesus of Nazareth.

You modeled the way you intended tradition
to inspire and instruct us as we partner with you
in our stewardship of the responsibilities
you have generated for us.
As you summarized that traditioning in the teachings of Jesus,
it improvises around loving you, loving others,
and loving ourselves
as you have loved us.
That's the swing into which you are drawing us
one conversation after another.

Wisdom in your traditioning of us in your service
allows for a more discerning dialogue
with those showing interest and engagement in acts of justice
that further your realization of your flourishing future.
In the records of your people's encounters with you,
this wisdom literature has been rooted in family systems
that have been a decisive in the handing on of your faith.
Through your wisdom,
you make us aware of the buoyancy and resiliency of your creation
as well as the right ways for us to work in caring for it with you.
The ancestors are our guides and guardians,
nourishing us to grow into our responsibilities
in our own times and places.
The wisdom that jazz plays
is the wisdom of the resilience
of your loving redemption of us
from all the traumas and tragedies that we experience.
Jazz conveys the deep tension
between our alienation and apprehension

and our joy and elation.
The resolutions, when they come, are astounding.

Effectiveness in your traditioning of us in your service
happens as you conduct the rich variety of gifts
we bring to the performance of our responsibilities
in contributing to your commonweal on earth and in heaven.
This is a communal endeavor.
The whole of humanity is your instrument.
Each of us, with all of our individuality and idiosyncrasies,
are summoned to contribute those to your service,
thus generating the sweet sounds of sanctifying significance
in and through all of us together.

Through the illuminating conversations
in which your Holy Spirit shapes our performances
in the dance halls of your delight,
make us instruments of your justice and peace.
Where there is hatred, provoke us to enhance your love.
Where there is offence, provoke us to enhance your pardon.
Where there is discord, provoke us to enhance your reconciliation.
Where there is error, provoke us to enhance your truth.
Where there is doubt, provoke us to enhance your faith.
Where there is despair, provoke us to enhance your hope.
Where there is darkness, provoke us to enhance your light.
Where there is sadness, provoke us to enhance your joy.

Attune us to where those gifts are manifest
most clearly and compellingly
in the stories of your encounters with your kin
down through the generations.
Enrich us with their contributions to our flourishing.

Improvisers embark on their personal odysseys with the conviction that they must share their talents with others, thus helping to maintain and ensure the survival of a unique, indispensable musical tradition. In so doing, they hope to make their mark on a world plagued by social conflict and preoccupied with materialistic values. Improvisers view performance as a positive force that can redress this imbalance, if only in a small way, by replenishing the earth's soundscape with music possessed of beauty and vitality, integrity and soul to remind listeners of these finer universal expressions of human aspirations.[45]

45. Berliner, *Thinking,* 503.

Prayer 36

Dear Family of Creator, your eighth freedom
is the freedom to organize our collaborations
with just enough structure
so we may work redemptively together.

It is your gift of creative orchestration.

The coordination revolves around your purpose
of forgiving and reconciling the world
so that all of us can bless each other.

The creativity emerges from the conversations we convene
in the process of coordinating.
They honor and benefit all the voices
participating in that composing
as both recipients and givers.

How are you arranging
the dynamic elements in that coordinating
so that contributors are drawn into the swing
of sanctifying significance?

I have contemplated the pattern of your constructive coordination
and found five qualities

that make them faithful, wise, and effective:
Soulful,
Mindful,
Astute,
Responsible, and
Trusting.

They form an acronym—SMART.
I usually refer to the pattern as SMARTer Conversations
to highlight your overall purpose of making things better.

I have put them in that order
because I think there is a sense to that flow
that draws together the deeply personal with the broadly communal.
They provide a framework for collaborating with you
in the reweaving of your intention,
as old patterns of relating to one another unravel.

The best model of your new ordering
that you have revealed
is a jazz band.

Let's explore how these dynamic elements
show up in the redemptive conversations
we convene in our partnership with you.

The Soulful conversations are the ones we have with ourselves
in our most honest and intimate times with you.
When you loosen our chains of suffering and shame,
you offer us a glimpse of the authentic partner
you intend us to be.

It is so easy to become lost
in the labyrinths of negative self-talk.
We become addicted to self-denigration.
Our traumas play on an endless loop,
over and over again to the point of defining us.

With gentle patience, you talk us out of our self-imprisonment.
You draw our attention to the gifts we have,
the capabilities with which you have entrusted us,
that enable us to join you in your reworking
of justice, peace, and joy
for the whole of your creation.

With that positive view as our focus,
the world looks different.
The embrace of your hospitality
frees us for innovative transformations.
Your gifts of dignity and worth
shine forth with hope and healing.

Our soul sings a new song of sanctifying significance.

The Mindful conversations are convened
on the strength of that humble confidence
that you are cultivating in our souls
when we practice sabbath with you.
At this moment the boldness of your vision for your creation
sends us out seeking the allies
you have already prepared for us
in the multitude of dance halls
where you have assigned us.

You awaken our attention to our kin
who have an inkling of what you are about in the world
and who have a hunch that there is authentic joy
in collaborating in generating the swing of your salvation.
As we improvise together in that missioning,
honing our unique contributions to the dance,
we mature into the corps of ambassadors
for your forgiving and reconciling love.

The Astute conversations shed light on
the contours of your potential.
This is the process of continually reformulating our faith
under the reliable illuminating of your Holy Spirit.
We analyze the situations.
We decide on the best approaches we can imagine together.
With compassion we strive for our best outcomes,
always open to the Spirit suggesting something different
as the conversation proceeds.

It is through these family consultations
that you have always worked the wonders of your revealing.
That's what is recorded in our scriptures.
The wisdom of the ancestors is honored,
the sufferings and pain of the present is confronted,
the promise of your commonweal is recognized,
and ways of contributing to it are imagined.

These are the chord charts of missioning with you.
They will always hit on the notes of faith, hope, and love.
They will always be rooted in the rhythms of grace and gratitude.
They will always generate dances of joy.

The Responsible conversations
shape how we will implement our decisions
relying on the best ways we can play our parts.
Through them, we assign roles and assure support.

We're not often well-coordinated in this part of the flow.
We're reluctant to impose accountabilities on others.
We're unskilled at providing support.
We get vague about our roles and just hope for the best.
That uncertainty can very quickly get dysfunctional and frustrating,
alienating us from each other in blame and shame.

The creative tensions between accountability and support
that are essential dynamics in good jazz.
They hold lessons we would benefit from learning.
There is a melody to be played.
There is a respect for the unique gifts everyone brings.
There is an appreciative reliance on each other.
There is an openness to adapting to new possibilities.
There is a commitment to making it feel good
for everyone in the dance hall.

The Trusting conversations,
paradoxically,
have to do with the processes of monitoring and measuring
how well the performance is accomplishing its purpose.

The effectiveness of a new clarity and effort
offer unimaginable benefits.
To what signs of success will we attend?

What indicators of achievement will we monitor?
What measures of improvement will we consider?

In the jazz community,
the monitoring and measuring have built up over the generations.
It is an accepted means of ensuring continual improvement.
There is an openness to honest assessment with mutual respect.
There is an appreciation for the benefits
that flow from this transformational process.
There is a commitment to provoking the best
in the performance of the group as a whole
for the delight of all in the dance hall.
There is a hope that the swing generated in the dance hall
will be carried into the networks
of all those making the dance happen.

We can all, by your mercy and grace, dear Family of Creator,
convene and craft conversations that align us in your service.

We can all, by your mercy and grace,
compose ourselves
soulfully, mindfully, astutely, responsibly, and trustingly,
one conversation after another.

We can all, by your mercy and grace,
cultivate the courage to be transformed
through these ongoing conversations
in ways that mature us into friendship with Jesus,
as players in his dance band.

Freedom for this kind of self-composition
is stifled when we are compelled to conform
to rigid rules and regulations
often thought necessary to control unruly humans.
Negativity about human potential dominates.

Seed your vision of a different way of being human together
so that it germinates through your musicking among us.

If we are to maximize performance, it is essential to employ just enough rules to afford autonomy, while at the same time avoiding chaos. Autonomy is the independence and freedom that enables people to act individually. It is necessary to foster the individual expression essential to both improvisation and innovation. Autonomy also facilitates agility, as it limits the constraints placed on individuals. All too often, people are swamped and forced to deal with conflicting priorities. Minimizing the number of rules helps to clearly dictate priorities and focus people on what really matters to the team. . . . Effective rules are limited to those that are necessary, that can be practically applied, and, above all, that are clearly defined, with each rule's importance adequately communicated.[46]

46. Cho, *Jazz Process,* 24.

Prayer 37

Dear Family of Creator, your nineth freedom
is the freedom to disrupt.
You challenge our patterns of thinking and acting
that create barriers to your work of redemption
for the whole of your creation.
You summon us to see things differently
so that we can mature in our partnership with you,
nourishing all your desires to flourish for our mutual delight.

There is a melody line for these disruptions.
They are not random.
They serve your vision of a flourishing creation
playing justice with kindness and humility.

Many of the ways we have devised to live together
are traumatizing,
inflicting violent suffering and pain.
This is true both personally and systemically,
individually and communally.
We are often too content and lazy
to examine these dynamics in the light of your mercy and grace.
Indeed, we are far too adept for our own good
at accepting these harmful dynamics,

especially if we are privileged by them
with power and prosperity.

You challenge us to repent,
to return to the partnership you created us for.
You open the door for that return through your forgiveness.
You welcome us with open arms through your reconciliation.

In the traditions of the jazz community,
mistakes are welcomed as a means of learning.
They are accepted as routine in performing with spontaneity,
noticed with a gentle attentiveness,
surrounded by supportive suggestions from colleagues,
examined for potential improvements,
then incorporated or left behind.

Within the context of your gift of mercy and grace,
we feel sufficiently safe
to be honest about our faults and failings.
We can go more deeply into the dynamics
that generate the ways we show up
in the networks where you call us to be blessings.
In the secure embrace of your forgiving love,
we can imagine boldly
new possibilities for returning
more faithfully, wisely, and effectively
to the family business of fostering flourishing.

Returning to your ways
will disrupt the ways we have arranged things
in our ignoring of you or our distortions of you.

Our certainties about the ways you have ordered creation
get challenged by your revelations
about how you are still choreographing
the moves you want to us to be making.

In the midst of our mess of mistakes,
you confront the pain of the way things are
with the joy of the way you want them to be.

When we take risks in serving you,
we are going to make mistakes,
no matter how competent we have become
in the use of our tools for serving you.
When we are serving you,
we trust you to turn those mistakes
into meaningful contributions.
When we find new meaning resulting from our mistakes,
we are engaged in composing of our sanctifying significance.

Awaken us further to the freedom of your forgiveness
in the service of your reconciling love.

The creativity of each new jazz performance is improvised on the jazz tradition. Jazz requires a step into the unknown, an interdependence with other musicians, in order to create something beautiful. Similarly, the biblical tradition should inspire fresh improvisations, daring creativity, interdependence, careful listening, and pursuit of beauty. The creativity demonstrated in the Scriptures themselves demands that we not merely re-perform Christian community (as in reading notes off a page) but improvise church, riffing on the biblical story within our neighbourhoods.[47]

47. Glanville, *Improvising Church*, 4.

Prayer 38

Dear Family of Creator, your tenth freedom
is the freedom to delight in the surprising ways
you are drawing us into the dance
that makes your creation flourish.

It is your gift of joy in our sanctifying significance,
in our goodness as your dance partners.

There is something about the music and the movement
in your choreography of our lives
that energizes the best of who we are
and aspire to be.

The layers of these rhythms
animate our deepest intuitions of dignity and worth.

What is the feel of those rhythms you lay down for us?
They feel like the heartbeat of our mother when we are in her womb.
They feel like the original blessing of our formation
in the pulsations of grace and gratitude.
They feel like original belonging as original blessing.
They feel like the vibes that connect us with all creation
in mutual obligation to choose life,
one conversation after another.

They feel like an invitation to live in creative communion
with the Source of all of life's vibrations.

The patterns of the melodies
inspire the flow of our steps
across the dance floor of your creation.

What are those melody lines that you suggest for us?
You have made us partners in forming your creation.
You have promised to be with us always so we can be blessings.
You have suggested possibilities that will guide us in that work.
You have inspired and instructed us,
generation after generation
through ancestors who have been embraced
by the truth of the kindness and humility of your justice.
You have summed up all those messages
in your invitation to love you, love others, and love ourselves.
Faith, hope, and love are your eternal gifts.
The greatest of these
is your forgiving and reconciling love.
That is the melody line
from which all the others derive
and to which the final resolution of all the tensions in the dance
will return.

The imaginings of the harmonies
that can be played and hummed throughout the dance
open up redeemed ways of understanding our relationship.

What is the influence of those harmonies
as they get composed in the dancing?

They awaken us to the multitude of possibilities
that you are generating for our flourishing with you.
They awaken us to the untold combinations of voices
that enrich our experimentations.
They awaken us to the importance of listening openly
for different ways of adding our voice to the emerging composition.
They awaken us to the benefits of adaptability
in collaborating to enhance the rhythms and melody lines.

In the traumatizing dynamics of life imagined
without a relationship with you
or in a relationship that impedes our ability to serve your intentions,
liberate us from the deadening despair
that envelops us when we try to make it without you.
Alert us to your workings among us
even when we don't acknowledge your presence.
Infuse our awareness with your musicking.
Bring us to deeper awareness that you are the source
of the swing of sanctifying significance in our lives.

As the dance goes on,
you call us into transformations
that ally us more fully
with your intentions for your creation.
You encourage and equip us
to be responsible citizens of your flourishing future,
revealed so clearly on that first Easter morning
when you enabled us to join you in the dance
and promised to live in us as we live in you.

> . . . [music is] a healing force . . . [that] transcends all political, social and ethnic barriers because it speaks directly to the heart. . . . My talent is a medical formula handed down from the creator. I am a dispenser of medicine.[48]

48. Berliner, *Thinking*, 825.

Prayer 39

Dear Family of Creator, the ten freedoms
you have explored with us
interweave and intermingle
in the musicking that inspires us to dance with you
in every breath that we take.

As we name them again,
awaken our ability to explore the possibilities
of how you are at work through them in our lives.

Your forgiving and reconciling love infuses
your freedom to hang out, to listen, to contribute,
to engage in dialogue, to unlearn and relearn, and to rely on others.
You open the tradition
to our reformulations, our collaborations,
our disruptions, and our delight.

Musicking of all kinds liberates our souls,
but there is a special sound of freedom in jazz.
It comes from the myriad oppressions
that brought the tradition to birth and shaped its maturing.

When we pay attention
to the interdependencies of these dynamics

in the daily flow of our lives,
as we move around the dance floor
one conversation after another,
we are open to the swing of the Family of Creator,
energizing the sanctifying significance
that blesses the whole of creation.

Martin Luther King Jr was caught up in this swing
when he paid tribute to the power of jazz in 1964
in his opening address at the Berlin Jazz Festival:

"Jazz speaks for life.
The Blues tell the story of life's difficulties,
and if you think for a moment,
you will realize that they take the hardest realities of life
and put them into music,
only to come out with some new hope or sense of triumph. . . .
Much of the power of our Freedom Movement in the United States
has come from this music.
It has strengthened us with its sweet rhythms
when courage began to fail.
It has calmed us with its rich harmonies
when spirits were down.
. . . in the particular struggle of the [Blacks] in America
there is something akin to the universal struggle of modern man.
Everybody has the Blues.
Everybody longs for meaning.
Everybody needs to love and be loved.
Everybody needs to clap hands and be happy.
Everybody longs for faith."[49]

49. King Jr, "Jazz."

When we recognize and ally with the life-giving energy
that draws us into the choreography of your mercy and grace,
we hook up and hang out with a bewildering variety of your kin.
Our freedoms from the confines and strictures of our old imaginings
sound forth and move freely towards
your flourishing justice, peace, and joy.

Ignite our appreciation of your freedoms
for our sanctifying significance.

The freedom to develop faithful communities in a particular context actually can allow people to find meaningful connection with wider traditions, both those belonging to the Christian faith and those of the community's ancestors or neighbors who were not Christians. In them, the community can learn to discern the healing, transformative work of the Spirit. . . . [For the Galatians, this] opened the door for much creativity and locally based solutions about how to follow Jesus in a given place and time. Any given culture will have both liberating and oppressive aspects that need to be deepened or transformed, as the case may be.

. . . Paul doesn't hesitate to denounce any thing that leads to the constricting of freedom in Christ, no matter what its pious garb. . . . A central hermeneutical principle then, for which Paul himself gives us the warrant, is that whenever he is quoted in a way that leads to the destruction of freedom in Christ, this should be pointed out, not submitted to "even for a moment" (Gal 2:5), lest the gospel be distorted.[50]

50. Bedford, *Galatians*, 8–9 & 42–42.

Third Movement

On Dancing Institutionally

Prayer 40

Dear Family of Creator, when you co-create communities with us,
you are moulding our contributions
into ecosystems of support
for the values you aspire to cultivate.
Through these values your network of kin
become ambassadors of your forgiving and reconciling love.

You are creating institutions with us.
You are cultivating respect-in-depth
for your community's ongoing conversations with our ancestors.
You are helping us to imagine faithful, wise, and effective innovations
in the ways we might dance better together
in your freedom.

Your manifest church, from its very beginnings,
has valued welcoming, worshiping, learning, and serving
as an embodiment of your mercy and grace.

Your unconditional hospitality
welcomes the return of all your kin.

Your celebration of those returns
helps us as we recognize and rejoice
in the dignity and worth

you have sowed deep in our souls
and nourishes us to engage in a liberated flourishing.

Your patience with our convoluted process
of learning, unlearning, and relearning
guides us to find our substance and sound
when we play for the swing dances of your salvation.

Your mysterious, illuminating influence
introduces us to the networks
where we can best serve together,
where our greatest passions might meet your world's greatest needs.
You invite us to be part of the pickup band
that joins with your Trinity Trio
to draw more and more people
into your dance of sanctifying significance.

What then might the church learn from jazz
that would enable us to hone our with-ness and witness
to improve the consistency
with which we willingly get into the groove of your swing?

In our institutional praxis of welcoming,
we might realize more delightfully
the resonance of God's intention of composing belonging
in every connection we make.

In our institutional praxis of worshiping,
we might engage more gratefully
in the regular communal rituals
of approaching, confessing, being called, and responding.

In our institutional praxis of learning,
we might discern more insightfully
where you are working your wonders
throughout your whole wide world.

In our institutional praxis of serving,
we might contribute more beneficially
for all those within our networks of inspiration and influence
whose pain and suffering
you have seen and heard
and brought to our attention.

There is in your institutional church
a patterned praxis, a choreographed dance,
that is your primary means of encouraging and equipping us
to be ambassadors of your swing.

Guide us into deeper considerations of those disciplines.

In time, I realized that jazz is more than a metaphor for organizing. Jazz bands actually are organizations designed for innovation, and the design elements from jazz can be applied to other organizations seeking to innovate. Further, in order for jazz bands to be successful, they require a commitment to a mind-set, a culture, practices and structures, and a leadership framework that is strikingly similar to what it takes to foster innovation in organizations.[51]

51. Barrett, *Yes,* x.

Prayer 41

Dear Family of Creator, in honing our welcoming
we see modeled in the dynamics of jazz
a curiosity about the complementary gifts to be found in others,
a respect for the potential in all of us for contributing,
a sensitivity to our pain and suffering,
an appreciation for what we are offering in each encounter,
an openness to being provoked by our playing,
a commitment to improvising new collaborations,
and a delight in the discoveries you reveal.

You created us to partner with you and others
in blessing your creation
by playing in bands of ambassadors
of your mercy and grace.
You planted in each of us a unique mix of knowledge and skills
to be cultivated for this purpose.
Give us the listening skills to imagine
how to best play with others,
to draw everyone into the swing of our sanctifying significance.
Conduct us in offering and developing those gifts
in the networks into which you send us.
Some of those networks are consciously practicing
faith, hope, and love in relationship with you.
Others are curious but cautious about such a commitment.

Others have been traumatized into rejection
because of misrepresentations of your activities.
Others yet have no inkling of your work among them.
Whatever the conditions we find,
provoke our curiosity,
help us to detect opportunities,
and to be instruments of the hope and healing
being generated by your unconditional hospitality.
Hone the sound and substance of our welcoming,
so it resonates faithfully, wisely, and effectively with yours.

You gave each of us capacities for contributing
to the swing of your salvation
as it flows throughout the earth and beyond.
The more respect we show for those boundless capacities,
the more willingness we have to share them.
When people are heard with respect,
they feel sufficiently safe to give of themselves
for the good of the whole.
The wounds of pain and suffering heal.
A more experienced and empathetic presence develops.
Confidence in contributing is nourished.
Potential goodness is imagined and realized.

Musicking is medicine for our sin-sick souls.
The mysterious complexities of evil
disrupt and destroy our lives.
They subvert our service with you.
You know our pain and suffering better than we do.
You hear our cries as we shiver in the shackles of sin.
You do not forsake us,

however much we may feel that you have.
Assure us that we can submit our traumas to you
in the hope of the healing
that comes through being with you
in playing your sweet swing of our sanctifying significance.

You delight in the gifts you give us.
You encourage and enable us to cultivate them in your service.
You appreciate when they come to fruition in our playing.
You join us together in joyful gratitude
for the benefits flowing through our dancing.
Make us thankful for the whole process of your musicking.
Alert us to the intricate interdependencies that make it all work.
Awaken us to our communal and personal capacities
for the empathy you have given us,
so that each dance number aligns us more fully
with the flow of your forgiveness and reconciliation.

Open our senses to what you are provoking in our playing.
Make us aware of the possibilities being called forth.
Cultivate in us creative collaboration
that realizes our potential for allying with your goodness.
Strengthen us to see mistakes as opportunities to learn.
Free us by forgiving us our foibles and failures
and enable us to respond in kind with each other.
Ignite our collective imagination with your new song.

Many of the tried-and-true ways of being your church
are no longer working.
The places to which you are sending us
as ambassadors of your mercy and grace

are filled with people who ignore or reject
your call to partnership in your redemption.
Our old ways of connecting, communicating, and committing
have become impotent.
We have become fixated on their maintenance.
Help us see the refreshing ways in which jazz bands
honor the traditions without being trapped in them.
Encourage us in improvising around the core values of your church
so that the fruits of your influence—
love, joy, peace, patience, kindness, generosity,
faithfulness, and gentleness—
will inform new configurations of your missioning.
Give us a humble confidence in our capacities for collaborating
with you and others
in playing the swing of your salvation.

Your welcoming gives us an enduring sense of belonging.
In the security of knowing we are loved by you,
we discover new ways to learn, contribute, and innovate
that surprise and delight us.
That joy becomes infectious with hope and healing.
Awaken us more fully to this dynamic
working among and through us
as your band of ambassadors.

Jazz is a culture that is both rich and varied, and yet somehow united. An important feature of that culture is not only the suffering and pain that is expressed in the music, but the intense joy—indescribable joy, a joy that is perhaps only capable of being articulated through music.[52]

52. Edgar, *Supreme Love*, 172.

Prayer 42

Dear Family of Creator, in honing our worshiping,
you draw us into a celebration of worthiness—yours and ours.

You call us to gather and welcome us
as worthy of partnership with you
in your work of reweaving the fabric of your good creation.

You draw us into the swing of your redeeming dances.
In your embrace, we acknowledge your worthiness
as our Creator, Redeemer, and Reformer.

You show us that we are able
to engage more fully
and that we are capable of more.
Where we have failed
you assure us we can do better.

You inspire and instruct us
as we engage in conversations
with our ancestors and our kin in the present
about possibilities for unlearning and relearning
the ways of being more worthy bands of ambassadors
for your forgiving and reconciling love.

We respond with rewoven commitments
arising from our reformed understandings
of our worth for your creation.
This flows from our regular rituals
that celebrate our mutual worthiness
in provoking greater love and more good works.

Awaken us to the intricacies
of the intimate choreography
by which you allure us more consciously
into the relationship you desire with us.
There is a bounce of joy in those moves.
Stir up the grateful glee we receive
in your forgiving friendship.

In the security of that renewing relationship,
we can be honest about ourselves with you
in candid confession about where we have failed you.
We can be opened to learning from our mistakes.
Perhaps we can even find in those mistakes
your suggestions for improvements.

As these intimate conversations in prayer
about the dynamics and flow of our relationship
draw to a close for the time being,
you reach out and embrace us with your assurance of pardon
and your support for our improving.

You follow that guarantee of grace
with conversations composed to ignite our imaginations.
We read the remembrances of our ancestors.

We consider generations of interpreters.
We reflect upon our own situations and contexts.
We envision possibilities
for more faithful, wise, and effective partnerships
as we disperse into the various networks
in which you are seeding us.
We compose engagements and enterprises to try
as ambassadors of your mercy and grace.

In the final steps of the dance of worshiping,
you invite us to devise ways of implementing
at least some of the steps we've learned
in our weekly dancing.
You refresh our understandings.
You renew our commitments.
You restore our humble confidence.
You send us out
to carry on the swing of your service
through the sanctifying significance
you have strengthened within us.

In this weekly ritual of worshiping,
you provide a rich seed bed
of community and consideration
in which to hone our praxis of our faith.

You get our toes tapping and our bodies moving
with the joy of your redeeming mercy and grace.

We have all likely been around a drummer playing and felt the reverberation in the whole room. We hear it and we feel it, and this drum on life becomes the composer of the beat of life. The vibrations connect us to each other. . . . The Spirit is vibration, as all things in our world have vibrations. This notion is an important concept to study as we try to navigate beyond the confines of Eurocentric and patriarchal models of understanding the Holy Spirit. This is another lens by which we can rethink and reimagine the Holy Spirit. Spirit as vibration moves us to take actions and initiatives now. The Spirit moves us into action as "vibration in action." Spirit as vibration accompanies us, empowers us, and stirs us to strive toward greater equity and justice.[53]

53. Kim, *Reimagining*, 86–87.

Prayer 43

Dear Family of Creator, in honing our learning,
focus our attention on smaller words that convey a larger wisdom—
"about," "in," "with," "of," "for," "by," and "so."

So much of our learning these days is "about" things.
We dissect from a distance
to figure out how it all works.
We dig into the past
to find our how it all started.
We pull together our findings
to discover how to control it all.

With this model of learning,
we too often approach you as the Thing that got it all started
and, perhaps, keeps it all going
by techniques that can be discovered and manipulated
for our personal or group benefit.

Getting into the swing of your divine dance
doesn't work that way.
Learning the choreography of your redeeming
is much more mysterious and disruptive
of our assumptions and preconceptions.

Joining you in the joy of jazz in the dance hall of your creation
is life-long learning at its most inspiring and invigorating,
a continuous process of maturing into our partnership with you.

There is the time of imitation.

You birth and rebirth us into communities
filled with other human beings
who have learned the basic moves of dancing with you.
We watch and listen.
We discern patterns and processes.
We repeat them as best we can.
We incorporate into the rituals and language
of those we respect and trust.
Love of these people
and loyalty to their ways
emerges "in" their company.

The arts of relating we learn are not perfect,
not by any stretch of the imagination.
We are learning from treasures in earthen vessels.
They are inspiring and instructing treasures in earthen vessels.
Patterns of arrogance and abuse are far too common
and far too lasting.
Pain and suffering accompany our learning
and deface your image in our relating.

But our imaginations never lose a sense of that image in us.
You are always at work pestering and provoking us
to assimilate and appropriate the best of your teachings
and incorporate them to co-compose

different ways of being together "in" and "with" you
"so" we can be more fully "for" you.

You activate our imaginations for liberating learning.
It is communal, transformative, and redemptive.
You honor our pain and suffering
but do not leave us imprisoned in them.
You make us blessings for others and our creation.

As we become more and more aware
of being embraced "by" your forgiving and reconciling love,
we come to know deeply the selves we are
"with" you and "for" you.

The more we assimilate and appropriate your mercy and grace
through our practicing and performing
the mysterious disciplines of life "with" you,
the more we grow into our authentic selves
"in" companionship with you and your kin.

Early on in the process of assimilating and appropriating,
we feel the urge to innovate,
to experiment with possibilities we imagine might work
"so" we can be more closely allied with what you are doing,
more in sync with the swing of your salvation.

We will make mistakes in our innovating.
They may be mistakes rooted in patterns from our past.
They may be mistakes we concocted all on our own in the present.
They may be mistakes that open up a new way into the future.
Whatever the configuration of these mistakes,

help our failures feed our flourishing
through your forgiving love.
Turn them into redemptive riffs of reconciliation.
Dance us into a different future
infused with the flow "of" your saving swing.

Awaken us to the dynamic of learning the sanctifying significance
of living "in" you and "for" your love of others
who bring their pain and suffering to your dance hall
"so" they will be healed "by" your hope.

First, jazz is self-consciously spontaneous, creative, and expressive. It is fundamentally concerned with inventiveness as an expected mode of thought and behavior. Second, jazz is most typically a social process, involving a group of inventive musicians. Jazz enables individual musicians to coordinate the innovation process so that that they achieve a credible and aesthetically pleasing collective outcome. The jazz process is built on the assumption that each individual musician is simultaneously and consciously adapting to the whole, supporting the other players, and mutually influencing the outcome. Jazz is thus a truly collective approach to the entire process of innovation, for it requires that the invention, adoption, and implementation of new musical ideas by individual musicians occurs within the context of a shared awareness of the group performance as it unfolds over time.[54]

54. Cho, *Jazz Process*, 9.

Prayer 44

Dear Family of Creator, in honing our serving,
draw our empathy to all those
in whom the light of your life shines.

Sharpen our seeing
to recognize more clearly the energy of your presence
in those who are considered least on this earth.

Tune our hearing
to perceive more fully their pain and suffering,
the aspirations for sanctifying significance
you have sown in their souls.

Stimulate our tasting
to pick up the bitter and the sweet of life
in the melange of misery and merriment
that we encounter in our networks.

Sensitize our smelling
to sniff out the sources of rot and decay
that prevent the fragrance of your transforming presence
from being known and enjoyed.

Enliven our touching
to encourage more boldly the beauty of belonging
in a society addicted to demeaning and dismissing.

Through all the senses you have gifted to us
in order to connect in compassion with other creatures,
nourish our resilience in serving your flourishing.

Each and every day, you take us into your world
and place us in networks
where opportunities emerge to serve your desire
for universal flourishing.
They may involve something as simple as a smile.
They may involve something as complex as system change.
They will all involve the humanizing/divinizing of our life together.

In all of our encounters,
ever maturing in our awareness of our friendship with you,
fill our engagement
with the toe-tapping, finger-drumming,
head-bobbing, and foot-sliding
that comes when we are musicking with you
in your dance halls and in their neighborhoods.

Our serving is, above all else, the dance of the prophets.
Their repertoire of saving songs,
sung into the miseries of their times and places,
became the playlist for Jesus and his band of followers.
Your first recorded sermon in his home town of Nazareth
picked up these riffs as played by Isaiah—
good news to the poor, release to the captives,

recovery of sight to the blind, freedom for the oppressed.
These are the fruits of your favor.
And, you said through Jesus on that day,
all of these things were being realized
in and through him.
Most of his old friends and neighbors from his home town
took offense—to the point of trying to kill him!
That offense is the costliness of dancing in your service.

Jazz, like Jesus, offends and frightens
those who want to keep you under tight control,
who want to compose rigid regulations
to keep out those who are different.

In the early days of jazz,
and even today in some networks,
jazz is seen as "the devil's music."
It is feared for being too wild and raucous.
It is denigrated for being
"a sick moment in the progress of the human soul."
It is heard as having "libidinous urgings" leading to
the "propulsive swagger" of the "sacred's absence."
It is heard as "barbaric, sensuous, jungle music
which assaulted the senses and sensibilities,
diluted reason, led to the abandonment of decency and decorum,
undermined dignity, and destroyed order and self-control."[55]
It is heard like the prophetic musicking that it is.

From our prophetic ancestors in all times and places,
give us their vision of your flourishing.

55. Bivins, *Spirits*, 10.

Awaken us through every sense that we have
to the possibilities for blessing each other and our environments
with the justice, peace, and joy that you desire for your creation.

Provoke faithful, wise, and effective improvisations
around the chord/core charts
you have composed and arranged through them.

[In exploring jazz and American religion] I am sounding out mutually echoing refrains, pointing to overlapping materials, interpolated themes, and shared longings. This is yet another reason why this book, while it examines dozens of individuals, looks away from jazz hagiography to a music taking shape in the thick of interactivity, local scenes, the realities of door gigs, the overarching canopy of racial prejudice, all of it present in notes played as in pieties cultivated. . . . looking at the complex floriculture of this music reveals that its sounds, creators, concerns, and communities capture and participate in and play back to some of the most central and engaging concerns of American religions.[56]

56. Bivins, *Spirits*, 20–21.

Postlude

A Reprise of the Possible Learnings

Prayer 45

Dear Family of Creator, let's compose a reprise
of the principal riffs on sanctifying significance
that you have sown in us
in these improvisations we have been playing
on our dignity and worth as instruments of your blessings.

These next few prayers will review
key insights that have emerged from these conversations.

Hopefully, they will also provoke new insights
that will carry further afield our discerning dialogue
about how jazz can inform
the reweaving of your church's missioning.

Of all the possibilities we have explored in these conversations,
four appear most provocative.
If considered more deeply in more networks,
these riffs offer lessons the church might learn from jazz.
They would get us more beneficially engaged
in the musicking you are generating in your divine dance halls.

The first riff on sanctifying significance
is that this whole dynamic
is composed, choreographed, and improvised

by you with your people.
It follows the patterns and processes that are evolving
in your redemption of your creation.
You draw us into your jazz dancing for our mutual delight.

The second riff on sanctifying significance
is that the patterned movements in your jazz dancing
engage every dimension of our beings,
at every level of our living
in the sanctifying significance
of blessing your creation.

The third riff on sanctifying significance
is that the dances—our movements to your music—
are composed around chord/core charts
that express your forgiveness and reconciliation.
The energizing of this musicking
nourishes and hones the capabilities you have given us
to take up the responsibilities
to which you summon us daily.

The fourth riff on sanctifying significance
is that there are patterns of providential collaboration
in the organizing of our life together.
They respect and dignify all who dance with you
in your dance halls and their neighborhoods.
To clarify those and get into sync with their benefits
is essential to the successful reweaving of the church
and its capacity for continual reformulation
through its communal spiritual disciplines.

The fifth riff on sanctifying significance
is that all of this is happening in manifest ways that we recognize
and in implicit ways that you are revealing to us.
In dancing to the improvisations of your Trinity Trio
and the other players you invite into the mix,
we are turned from the isolating delusions of our daily lives
to be inspired and instructed by your mercy and grace.

This is a maturing process of practice and performance,
improving our use of your gifts
in turning mistakes into possibilities for blessing.

You are composing and choreographing
new tunes and movements continually
that will align us more fully with you and others
in co-creating your commonweal.

Awaken us more fully to this dynamic
in which you have us participating
and to which you desire that we contribute.

> . . . jazz improvisation should be seen as a hopeful and empowering activity. It models individual actors as protean agents capable of changing the shape and flow of events. In this sense, jazz holds an appreciative view of human potential: it represents belief in the human capacity to think freshly, to generate novel solutions, and to create something new and interesting, perhaps even transformative. All leaders and organizations should aspire to such a view.[57]

57. Barrett, *Yes*, 184.

Prayer 46

Dear Family of Creator, the first riff on sanctifying significance
is that this whole dynamic is generated by you with your people.
You draw us into your jazz dancing for our mutual delight.

It's hard for us to imagine relationships
in which there is direction without imposition,
where flourishing is moved to a deeper level
by suggestion rather than command,
where openness to co-creating is the aspiration.

But that is the kind of relationship
you intend us to have with you as partners in your salvation.
It is a partnership in SHALOM,
in the making of a peace that surpasses understanding
in its depth and breadth.
In the life, death, resurrection, and ascension
of Jesus of Nazareth,
in whom you inaugurated a new humanity,
you revealed the arts of relating
that are composed and arranged into the SHALOM—
love, joy, peace, patience, kindness, generosity,
faithfulness, and gentleness.
The dance you are choreographing for us has three basic steps—
justice, kindness, and humility.

The combinations of these arts and steps are endless,
but our improvisations always revolve around them.

In all of the playing that we do in all of our networks,
keep awakening us more fully
to your forgiving and reconciling initiatives
and your collaborative direction.

Deepen our appreciation for our capabilities
to partner with you,
even in our missteps and mistakes.

Energize us, encourage us, and educate us
to explore the possibilities you generate for us
to be better bands of ambassadors of your mercy and grace.
Inspire and incite us to practice our gifts
before and after every performance.

Major barriers to this kind of Christian imagination
and to the nourishment of our communities
come from the names you have given them.
They arise from our imperial ancestors.
Such hierarchical misrepresentations,
like "King," "Lord," and "Master,"
distort our understanding of your desired relationship,
that of "Family," "Friends," and "Partners."

You work is collegial, not commandeering.
Your suggestions, urgent though they may be at times,
open up possibilities rather than impose prescriptions.

All of these arts in relating
can be seen in the wit, workings, and wisdom of a jazz band
playing in a dance hall where belonging is glimpsed and nourished.

They are not perfect.
But they do give us a sense
of how being church differently
might generate new compositions
of our Family of Creator's eternal love songs
in the key of forgiveness and reconciliation.

What you, dear Family of Creator, are provoking
is listening with respect,
exploring with curiosity,
appreciating with anticipation,
and doing with courage.

Bring more fully to our awareness
ways of playing with each other
that expand our consciousness of your work in our networks,
that clarify ways of contributing more constructively to your work,
and that enhance the positive consequences of our partnership.

Focus our attention on the possibilities you generate
in our welcoming, worshiping, learning, and serving
in our particular dance halls, neighborhoods, and communities.

Free us from the need to copy others.
Free us for the enjoyment
of our unique compositions and arrangements.

Jazz exemplifies artistic activity that is at once individual and communal, performance that is both repetitive and innovative, each participant sometimes providing that ground support and sometimes flying free.[58]

58. Bateson, *Composing*, 2–3.

Prayer 47

Dear Family of Creator, the second riff on sanctifying significance
is that the patterned movements in your jazz dancing
engage every dimension of our beings
at every level of blessing your creation.
Submitting to the swing of this salvation
catches us up in the flow of flourishing
that serves the welfare of our whole world.
We dance for justice with kindness in humility.

What patterns have you guided us into
in order to nourish our flourishing
as ambassadors of your forgiving and reconciling love?
What dance steps keep us in sync
with your intention of blessing your creation?

In a culture deluded by materialism and individualism,
you show up in community, with community, and for community.
You are, in your very self, a community.
You created us to be a partnering community with you.
You are engaged in the enterprise of building community
for all the inhabitants of earth and beyond.

The patterns of provoking in which you show up
all express the communal chord of your intentions.

You welcome us in ways that awaken us to our right to belong.
In the security of belonging with you and each other
in your family business of redemption,
we are freed for being drawn together as we are
and being transformed and dispersed as you are maturing us to be.

You worship with us as we celebrate our mutual dignity and worth.
We do not need to keep up any false fronts,
put on airs, or try to impress.
In being honest with you about the stage of our maturing,
about our wanderings in the deserts of our despair,
about our follies and failures in trying to be gods,
you open up for us possibilities for more faithful flourishing.
Our worshiping becomes a feast of sanctification
in our significance for blessing your creation.

You are with us as we learn the arts of relating
that compose your new humanity,
inaugurated and modeled in Jesus of Nazareth, your Christ.
Part of the image of you that we bear in our genes
is that curiosity to discover how things might be better.
How can we work together to improve things?
How can we recognize the possibilities for vibrant living
that you have sown in the killing fields
in which we find ourselves?
We look for the signs of your mercy and grace
in the struggling sprouts of your
love, joy, peace, patience, kindness, generosity,
faithfulness, and gentleness.
We cultivate those sprouts into the garden of your delights,
dancing all the while with you.

You draw us into networks where stress injuries abound,
where you think our faith and wisdom
can be effective in sounding your hope and healing
among all those with whom we are living.
You cultivate among us a resilience
in with-nessing and witnessing
that strengthens our patient persistence
in contributing to the musicking of your salvation.

Out of these communal spiritual disciplines,
you nurture unique personal ways
in which we can stay in the swing
of your providential musicking.
You draw us into the delights
of prayer, of pondering the scriptures,
of conversing with our ancestors in our traditions,
of considering with each other the possibilities we discover
to reformulate those traditions according to your illumination,
of trying out improvisations,
rejecting some and incorporating others
in our family dances.

Persuade us of the deep benefits
that flow from practicing and performing
these spiritual disciplines
in ways appropriate to the sounds and substance
through which we contribute our selves
as your band of ambassadors.

Cultivate in us a deep appreciation
for the structural configurations of playing together

that work best in allying and aligning us as partners
in your enterprise of redemption.

Keep us challenging these processes constructively
to improvise new compositions, arrangements, and moves
that will spread the inspiration and influence
of your gifts of belonging and blessing.

Utilize the lively flourishing
of our forgiving and reconciling love
to draw others into the musicking
of your salvation for your world.

[Jazz] becomes a way of life, and how you relate musically is really involved. The selfish or shallow person might be a great musician technically, but he'll be so involved with himself that his playing will lack warmth, intensity, beauty and won't be deeply felt by the listener. He'll arbitrarily play the first solo every time. If he's backing a singer he'll play anything he wants or he'll be practicing scales. A person that lets the other guy take the first solo, and when he plays behind a soloist plays only to enhance him, that's the guy that will care about his wife and children and will be courteous in his everyday contact with people.[59]

59. Gottlieb, *Reading Jazz*, 278.

Prayer 48

Dear Family of Creator, the third riff on sanctifying significance
is that our dances to your music
are composed around chords
that infuse us with your forgiveness and reconciliation.
The energizing of this musicking
nourishes and hones the capabilities you have given us
to take up the work
to which you summon us daily.

There are eight notes
that combine into the chords of your SHALOM—
love, joy, peace, patience, kindness, generosity,
faithfulness, and gentleness.
The feel of flourishing that your improvising generates,
the swing of sanctifying significance
that flows from composing and arranging with those notes,
is being just
with empathy
in humility.

The networks into which you send us,
vibrating with the energy of your dance halls,
are infected with fearfulness, laziness, and self-righteousness.
This toxic mix conspires to divide us from each other.

We find a false and fleeting security
in demeaning and dismissing those who are different from us.
We traumatize them with the violent imposition
of our way of seeing and doing things.

Awaken us to the many ways this is happening,
often subtle but pervasive,
always subverting your intentions for your creation.

Make us agents in your subversion of our falseness.
Guide our imaginations into your groove of blessing.
Move our interactions into your swing of sanctifying significance.
Introduce our potential into your redemptive reweavings.

Mentor us continually in your ways of making this all happen.
You are a crucified God whose "throne" is a cross.
You are a suffering servant who hangs out
with the rejected and the reviled.
You are a listener to the pain of your peoples.
You are a welcoming parent for those who have wandered.
You are a forgiving friend.
You are the host at our banquet of reconciliation.
You are the steady and imaginative leadership team
that enlists, equips, and encourages us all
into the family business
to sow the seeds of your future,
no matter what the terrain or the cost.
You are the dance hall owner,
welcoming all who come at the door every night,
in the hope that redemptive connections will be made
that transforms a deep sense of despair
into an even deeper assurance of sanctifying significance.

See, if you put a musician in a place where he has to do something different from what he does all the time, then he can do that—but he's got to think differently in order to do that. He has to use his imagination, be more creative, more innovative; he's got to take more risks. He's got to play above what he knows—far above it—and what that might lead to might take him above the place where he's been playing all along, to the next place he's going, and even above that! So then he'll be freer, will expect things differently, will anticipate and know something different is coming down. I've always told the musicians in my band to play what they know and then play above that. Because then anything can happen, and that's where great music happens.[60]

60. Davis, *Miles*, 220.

Prayer 49

Dear Family of Creator, the fourth riff on sanctifying significance
is that there are patterns of providential collaboration
in the organizing of our life together.
They respect and dignify all who move with you
in your dance halls and their neighborhoods.
To bring the benefits of your rhythms into a new sync
is essential to the successful reweaving of the church
and its capacity for continual reformulation
through its communal practices.

To sustain and enhance improvisation and collaboration
for the well-being of your creation,
there are patterns of behavior that might be implemented
to optimize the possibility of successful performance.
They are,
in a flow that mirrors a great jazz performance:
listening with respect,
responding in timely and constructive ways,
appreciating all contributions,
suggesting improvements in the partnering,
testing out the possibilities with each other,
learning from our mistakes,
and integrating what is being learned
into the next moment of the performance.

In the language of my ancestors and colleagues
within The Presbyterian Church in Canada,
it's the continual reformulation of our understanding
of our participation in the ministry of Jesus Christ
under the continuing illumination of the Holy Spirit.

Listening with respect
works best if we bring to the conversation
a deep conviction that we are hearing the voice of God
in the speech of the other,
no matter who that other may be.
In every conversation, the image of God,
in which we have been created as community,
is finding expression through everyone involved.
We do not partner with our Family of Creator
through monological messaging.
We play our parts most constructively
through dialogical discernment.

Responding in timely and constructive ways is essential
if the momentum of the swing is to be sustained.
In the rhythms of grace and gratitude.
Too much of a gap in responding
disrupts the flow of the dance
by putting us out of sync with each other.
If the reaction is negative and critical,
it brings the flow of cooperation to a halt,
pushing people away rather than drawing them together.
As we co-create the church, one conversation after another,
the impulse and inspiration to make things better

is greatly enhanced by assuming the responsibility
of furthering the conversation promptly and positively.

Appreciating all contributions to the collaboration
is the lubricant
that keeps the contributors working together positively.
It involves expecting the best of others, and ourselves.
It involves looking for what is working well and improving that.
It means correcting dysfunctions that are disrupting that swing.
Such gratitude generates engagement and enjoyment
in achieving our collective purpose.

Suggesting improvements in the partnering
can get tricky in the heated passions of the performance.
Even, or perhaps especially, with the intention of making it feel good
for all involved,
we can get stuck in a stubborn insistence
that our way is best.
It's hard to hear alternatives.
It feels like a personal attack.
It comes across as demeaning and dismissing.
Our ego fears insignificance
and puts up a wall of self-righteousness.
The partnering is ruptured.
The performance is discordant.
You undermine the problematic walls that divide us
with your forgiveness and reconciliation.
Make us attentive to that influence
drawing us back together
into the swing of your salvation.

Testing out the possibilities with each other
brings your kindness and humility
more consciously into the dynamics of our interdependencies.
It opens us to a variety of options.
It calls forth from us a teachable spirit
that wonders what might be possible
beyond the bastions of our fears of being mistaken.
It cultivates attitudes and behaviors
that welcome diverse views on the best ways forward
to enhance the experience of the denizens of the dance hall
as they gather and disperse.
It generates new formulations of our life together.

Learning from our mistakes
means being open to transformations
in the ways we see the world and contribute to its flourishing.
When our take on the right way to do things
does not work out for the best,
analyzing the factors involved
and doing things differently
with as little judgement as possible
opens up a new future for a different quality of cooperation.
We get to know each other
in order to better complement and support each other.
We follow our Family of Creator's way
of forgiving and reconciling
for the well-being of all creation.

Integrating what is being learned
into the next moment of the performance
involves paying attention to the dynamics going on now.

We do co-compose our institutions
one conversation after another.
Every interaction matters
and we are only one breath away from making things better.
But we are being called to take that breath
and make the improvements best suited to our common purpose.
Every institution has a chord chart for that purpose.
We often call it the culture.
It's the way we collaborate to achieve our sanctifying significance.
If it is clear and has broad buy-in,
it frees us for contributing.
If it is vague and uncertain,
it traps us in contention.
Open our souls to the swing of your salvation
in which you reveal to us the improvisations we might contribute.
Guide us to find and follow these patterns
in all the communal disciplines
into which you draw us—
welcoming, worshiping, learning, and serving—
and to incorporate them into the ways we show up
in your dance halls and their neighborhoods.

> Creativity needs to be examined as a system, not as isolated initiatives. The goal is to understand how all the variables fit together. Done properly, the [creative] audit can lead to a complete revolution in how creativity is conceived and a plan of action implementing it. It should be a collaborative effort, for part of the audit's job is to raise awareness.[61]

61. Kao, *Jamming*, 173.

Prayer 50

Dear Family of Creator, the fifth riff on sanctifying significance
is that all of this is happening
in ways manifest and implicit that you reveal to us.
In dancing to the improvisations of your Trinity Trio
and the other players you invite into the mix,
we are turned from the isolating delusions of our daily lives
to be inspired and instructed by your mercy and grace.

This is a maturing process of practice and performance,
improving our use of our gifts
to turn mistakes into possibilities for blessing.

Repentance is a process of turning to partner with you.
It happens through our conversations with you and each other
about the flourishing of your creation.
These are different conversations
from the ones we hear and contribute to around us
in much of our daily lives.
These are conversations that bring to realization
the sanctifying significance
you have sown within us at our birth.
We are created and continually summoned to become
partners in the musicking of your dance halls.
They inspire and instruct everyone

who is drawn into the rhythm of your swing
and understands what it means to be of importance
in blessing your world.

To be constructive and cooperative,
the sound and substance of these conversations
are best imagined and expressed in curiosity.

What would you like to see happen?

What benefit do you see us getting from that?

What is most valuable to you in that benefit?

What is most valuable to us in that benefit?

Can we explore any differing values?

Can we align around the common ones
and agree to explore how the different ones
can enrich the effectiveness of the enterprise?

What is likely to interfere with us realizing the benefit?

Can we imagine removing any of these barriers?

How will we navigate the more difficult barriers?

What are the best ways to avoid criticism and contention,
and practice constructive consideration?

How will we analyze and rectify mistakes?

How will we celebrate the maturing
that generates sanctifying significance
for all engaged in the enterprise?

As we compose and arrange these sounds,
sacred energy will emerge from our collaborations.
Some of it will be familiar,
but might sound different.
Some of it will be strange,
but will resonate with our aspirations sufficiently
to generate experiments with it.
Your energizing Muse will provoke us
to new levels of appreciation for what has gone before
and new prospects for doing our missioning better.

Continue to draw our attention back to your intentions.
Encourage us to take the risks of improvising
that seem to hold out the promise of maturing
in our sanctifying significance.
And make it feel good for all involved,
so good that others want to join us in the play of your dancing.

The message Duke [Ellington] wanted to deliver [in his sacred concerts] consisted of his own beliefs about God, which were rooted in Christian doctrine but idiosyncratically selected and interpreted. The medium was his music, often paired with lyrics of his own making, and enhanced by dance and narrative. And it was *his* music—and his musicians, who employed the range of sounds at their command. The methods used were similar to those he employed in other creative activity. He collaborated. He was attentive to individual gifts and allowed for improvisation. Within his encompassing vision and meditative creative process, many different elements were brought together, modified, and transformed into something original and new.[62]

62. Steed, *Ellington*, 133–35.

Prayer 51

Dear Family of Creator,
what a wild and wonder-filled set of dances!
As we have moved around the dance floor of your missioning,
we have been stretched and strengthened
in our trust in and loyalty to you.
We have incorporated into our flow of partnering with you
new rhythms of movement,
new melodies of understanding,
and new harmonies of relating
with all your kin in your creation.

But, as always, you have opened up more for us.
You have suggested possibilities
that might align us more fully with your work
as your ambassadors
for your forgiving and reconciling love.

Your ways of infusing and influencing us
fascinate us and incite our curiosity.
They confront us with responsibilities.
They raise more questions
for our developing flourishing.

Here are five that I will continue to explore
in these morning conversations in prayer with you
and pay attention to as we dance through our days.

Let's frame them around a seminal drone line
that underlies all of our prayers so far.
That drone line is "sanctifying significance."

What would we add to our sanctifying significance if
we considered others we meet
as conversation players and jazz musicians
who bring gifts from you to our missioning and musicking?

We might see treasures
in the midst of our collective traumas.
They might energize our earthiness
into a companionship and collaboration
that brings the blessing of belonging
in hope and healing.

We might find ourselves caught up in the swing of your salvation.

What would we add to our sanctifying significance if
we surrendered to the gracious groove
of your forgiving and reconciling love
one conversation after another?

We might form alliances
that arrange and compose suites of sacred sense,
that draw us together in clarity and courage
for the reformulation and reweaving of our living together.

We might find ourselves caught up in the swing of your salvation.

What would we add to our sanctifying significance if
we accepted with kindness and humility
the frailties and foibles of our allies
in our family business of caring for your creation?

We might take the worst of mistakes as learning opportunities
to become more attuned
to your presence in our lives,
to become more awakened
to the possibilities for improvement you offer,
to become more aligned
with your processes of redeeming.

We might find ourselves caught up in the swing of your salvation.

What would we add to our sanctifying significance if
we appreciated deeply the impact we were having
on the dynamics in your dance halls
and the ways that energy spreads from there
throughout your world?

We might come to see ourselves
as belonging in your corps of ambassadors
serving your mercy and grace in all we do.
We might recognize more deeply
that you saw us as valued contributors
to the cultivation of your justice
with a courage, a kindness, and a humility
modeled for us in Jesus of Nazareth, your Christ.

We might find ourselves caught up in the swing of your salvation.

Would we add to our sanctifying significance
if we developed the discipline of surrender
to your swing of SHALOM?

Could we compose our entire lives
around the grace notes of
love, joy, peace, patience, kindness, generosity,
faithfulness, and gentleness?
Those compositions would bring the suites of SHALOM
to your shamed and suppressed people.
They would encourage and equip them
to rediscover their sanctifying significance
in playing and dancing with
the bands of blessing you infuse with your inspirations.

Could we find ourselves caught up in the swing of your salvation?

To imagine your church, manifest and latent,
as dance halls energized by jazz bands
may well seem discordant and disruptive
to the ways we currently understand how church should be.

That's because it is.

But in the discord and disruption of improvisation,
with the energy of your forgiving and reconciling love,
renewed faith, renewed hope,
and renewed ways of being ambassadors of your love,
we might emerge from our reformulations

with a better understanding
of how best to serve as your ambassadors.

Provoke among us and in us more questions
that open up more possibilities
for adding to our sanctifying significance.

And encourage us to share those questions with each other,
one conversation after another.

Jazz is conversation. The art of civility. It is knowing when you've said enough, and not talking when you've nothing to say. It is being careful to not ignore other people's opinions. It is practicing hospitality, making room for others.[63]

63. Des Cotes, *Jazz Is*, 8.

Deep Gratitude

Prayer 52

Dear Family of Creator, no other art form
generates as much exuberant appreciation as jazz.
Throughout the performances,
after each solo contribution
complemented by the whole group,
the audience applauds
and adds their sounds of "Yeah"! or "Nice"! or "Cool"! or "Ahhhh"!
Throughout the musicking,
there is a deep sense of gratitude and anticipation
for what will be revealed and discovered
in the improvisations of the performance and response.

It took a life-time of networking
to write this book.
It remains a work in progress.
This is a performance
played at a dance hall
on that pilgrimage.

I pray that the Spirit will generate
through these prayers and their phrasings
new insights and possibilities
in old networks of provocation and improvision

and will open up new opportunities for such missioning
in networks not yet imagined.

Here are some expressions of gratitude
for those networks of which I am most aware at this point.

For my family of origin
and the families that welcomed me in
through the joys and sorrows of three marriages.

For the Christian congregations,
those fellowships of the friends of Jesus,
that have nourished my families and me to flourish:
Drummond Hill, Niagara Falls, ON;
Knox, Georgetown, ON;
Rosedale, Toronto, ON;
Knox College, Toronto School of Theology;
St. Andrew's, Merritton, ON;
Sonya and Nestleton, ON;
Glebe, Toronto, ON;
St. Andrew's Hall and Vancouver School of Theology, UBC;
Kerrisdale, Vancouver, BC;
West Vancouver, BC;
Central, Vancouver, BC; and
Brentwood, Burnaby, BC.
All, in multiple and marvellous ways, enriched
my faithfulness, wisdom, and effectiveness
in our praxis of Christianity.

A special depth of gratitude
goes to the contributors to Brentwood's missioning,
especially in our companioning with the jazz community.

Knowing full well that I am leaving out many names, here are some who I treasure in my memories:

Margaret and Alex Fraser; Janet and Janet McDougall; Bill McKeown; Grey Eakin; Allan Farris; David Hay; Brian Ruttan; Ken Craigie; Kathleen Copeland; Remmelt Hummelen; Stuart Coles; Eilert Frerichs; Jim Estes; Trevor Wigney; Rick Alway; Gordon Haynes; Hans Kouwenberg; John Webster Grant; John Moir; Ramsay Cook; Keith Clifford; Geoff Johnston; Brian Clarke; Stuart Macdonald; Gord Turner; Tom Gemmell; Bill Klempa; Eoin MacKay; Joe McLelland; Ian Victor; Don Corbett; Rod Ferguson; Ted Siverns; Phyllis Airhart; Gerald Hobbs; David Lochhead; Doug Hall; Art Van Seters; Terry Anderson; Bud Phillips; Ian McKenzie; Helen Anderson; Bill Walker; Keith Brown; Norah Lewis; Cathy Sosnowsky; Woldy Sosnowsky; Nancy Farran; Paul Myers; Margaret Mullin; Mary Fontaine; Janette McIntosh; Jim Czegledi; Doug DuCharme; Renata Pratt; Roger Hutchinson; Bill Davis; Bill Phillippe; Kay Phillippe; Cory Weeds; Bill Weeds; Miles Black; Paul Rushka; Jon Bentley; Lorraine Foster; Tom Reynolds; Peter Woods; Gary Patterson; Nelson Boschman; Diane Lines; Tony Chamberlist; Ron Kinders; Rhian Walker; Gerry Teichrob; Dan Reynolds; Ben MacRae; Phil Murray; Scott Turnbrook; Judith Hardcastle; Roy Salmond; Glen Soderholm; Glen Inglis; Charles Burns; Jim Cruickshank; Charles Fensham; Sarah Travis; Mary Fontaine; Cal MacLeod; Laurie MacKay; Bruce Cairnie; Rob Fennell; Russ Daye; Kayden Gorden; Tyler Murray; Noah Franche-Nolan; Sophia Avelino; Giselle Rocha; Josh Santos; Adele Wilding; Darlene Cooper; Bill Sample; Marcus Mosley; Sandra Nixon; Monica Risborough; Matt Brough; Carmen Lansdowne; Jason Byassee; Ross Lockhart; Rebecca Simpson; Richard Topping; Dave MacQuarrie; Greg Freedman; Marilyn Norry; Victoria Campbell; Neale Bacon; Pam Wong; Winston Reckord; Emmanuel Boadu; Rita Long; Edrina Clarke; Will Clarke; Lynne MacNaughton; Amanda Currie; Ryk Brown; Earl McKenzie; Mike Allen; Conrad Good; Mike Bjella; Adam Cormier; Simon Millerd; Michael Wagler; Mark Bender; Pat Dutcher-Walls; Melanie Adams; LJ Mounteney; Mark Glanville; Natalia Pardalis; Lynn Szabo; Linda Szentes; Rick Reynolds; Mary Reynolds; Vonnie Hawkes; John Hawkes; Bruno Hubert; Kristian Braathen;

Nick Apivor; Dalannah Gail Bowen; Michael Creber; Jim Tinkess; Ruth Tinkess; John Whitehead; Joan Mariacher; Andrew Nemr; Bryn Kinders; Barry Morris; and Ron Dart.

A special depth of gratitude
goes to John Wellwood,
who did an amazing service
in suggesting detailed edits of the manuscript,
all the folks at Wipf and Stock, and Lianne Biggar.

I can't really comprehend
the hours I have spent listening to jazz
on recordings and live.
I do know I am attracted to jazz trios,
especially the classic piano trios
of Oscar Peterson, Monty Alexander,
Dan Reynolds, and Noah Franche-Nolan.

My deepest gratitude, under the great canopy of your mercy and grace,
goes to my wife, Jill Alexander,
my most intimate friend for the last 25 years.
Her love of jazz, depth of intuition, and breadth of compassion
continue to inspire and instruct me
one conversation after another.
She is the dearest hummingbird I have encountered
on our journey of spiritual healing.

The basic beat in and from your dance halls,
dear Family of Creator,
is that of grace and gratitude.

Keep deepening and broadening
the draw of that swing
among us, in us, and through us,
until your intentions for your creation
are fully realized.

Respect and trust: these are the things jazz teaches. When you listen to great musicians, you hear the respect they have for one another's abilities; after all, rhythm section excluded, musicians always spend more time listening than playing. And, rhythm section included, you see the trust they have for one another because they are always making adjustments in response to what someone else has just created. In the simplest and most essential context, creativity and innovation reiterate the importance of soul. They are, separately and together, an expansion of feeling and a supreme expression of our humanity. We have an artistic imperative to understand and reengage creativity and innovation, not merely for economic growth but as tools for democracy and accomplished citizenship. We have a cultural imperative to find common ground even with our fiercest competitors . . . and to play with integrity.[64]

64. Marsalis, *Higher Ground*, 165–66.

The Learnings So Far and Questions to Go Further

Belonging Together

Becoming aware of our belonging
in the musicking community of our Family of Creator,
provoked at so many levels of our being by jazz,
transforms the ways we show up in the world.

What attitudes and behaviors, then,
is the Spirit of the Creator's Christ
provoking among those with whom you are missioning
that might transform the belonging you are offering?

Listening for/to our Family of Creator

Being attentive to the ways that God
(the Spirit of the Creator's Christ)
is communicating with us in order to draw us further
into the sanctifying significance of replenishing the world
with the wonders of forgiveness and reconciliation.

What attitudes and behaviors, then,
is the Spirit of the Creator's Christ
provoking among those with whom you are missioning
that might draw you further into the praxis
of our Family of Creator's forgiveness and reconciliation?

Comping Each Other

Recognizing that in that belonging and listening
we are partnering with God
in allying with a diverse community of others
who bring their unique gifts
into the family business of a caring for creation,
gifts that complement ours
and are intended to be coordinated
in a constructive collaboration
for the flourishing of all involved.

What attitudes and behaviors, then,
is the Spirit of the Creator's Christ
provoking among those with whom you are missioning
that might generate a more faithful, wise,
and effective collaboration
that might contribute to a more faithful, wise,
and effective church?

Telling Love Stories

Jazz at its best, like church at its best,
explores our limitless potential,
gifted to us by our Family of Creator,
to compose love stories
that generate the swing of sanctifying significance
for the whole human species.

What attitudes and behaviors, then,
is the Spirit of the Creator's Christ
provoking among those with whom you are missioning
that might enhance the loveliness and liveliness
of your story telling?

Improvising the Future

Our Family of Creator invites us
into a life of continuous improvisation,
modeled in the workings, wisdom, and wit of jazz,
in finding the most faithful, wise, and effective ways
to be ambassadors of their forgiving and reconciling love
for the whole world,
manifest in particular configurations of talents
playing for particular audiences
seeking God's hospitality, hope, and healing.

What attitudes and behaviors, then,
is the Spirit of the Creator's Christ
provoking among those with whom you are missioning
that might free up your collective gifts
for exploring and experimenting with new ways
of cultivating a flourishing future?

Engaging in God's Business

The praxis of jazz at its best, as of church at its best,
engages people in a process of call-and-response
in which every voice
is honored, supported, challenged, and transformed
as the trajectory of human history is transformed
to generate justice and kindness with humility.

What attitudes and behaviors, then,
is the Spirit of the Creator's Christ
provoking among those with whom you are missioning
that might generate the compassionate courage
to invite every voice to contribute to changing the world?

Contributing to SHALOM

To align with the Spirit of the Creator's Christ
in contributing God's intent
of cultivating deep well-being for all creation,
leadership in church and jazz is entrusted with the responsibility
of creating space for a redemptive musicking to happen
for the delight of all involved.

What attitudes and behaviors, then,
is the Spirit of the Creator's Christ
provoking among those with whom you are missioning
that might generate the blessings of peacemaking
in all your networks?

Conversing for Collaboration

The conversations that generate jazz at its best,
like those that generate church at its best,
are compassionate, candid, and constructive
in exploring ways of improving
our unique and interdependent contributions
to the divine Family's business of caring for creation.

What attitudes and behaviors, then,
is the Spirit of the Creator's Christ
provoking among those with whom you are missioning
that might provoke constructive conversations
that generate more justice with kindness and humility?

Honoring the Ancestors

The rituals and reflections of the church's traditions
of welcoming, worshiping, learning, and serving
have been honed over many generations by our ancestors.
They provide just enough structure and sense
for us to work together in innovative ways
to meet the needs of our generations
with the gifts of the Creator's Christ's Spirit
love, joy, peace, patience, kindness, generosity,
faithfulness, and gentleness.

What attitudes and behaviors, then,
is the Spirit of the Creator's Christ
provoking among those with whom you are missioning
that might awaken us to the rich wisdom of our ancestors
as we improvise in reweaving the strands
of the church's best traditions?

Focusing on Sowing and Cultivating the Seeds

The ways in which the influence of jazz, as of church,
spreads throughout the networks
of those playing those art forms
are mysterious in their wondrous workings,
but they are hindered or prevented
if the players do not offer their best
in the sowing and cultivating,
then play above that.

What attitudes and behaviors, then,
is the Spirit of the Creator's Christ
provoking among those with whom you are missioning
that might draw our attention to new fields
where we can sow and cultivate your seeds
of sanctifying significance?

Enjoying the Dance of Divine Delight

Jazz bands at their best, as church at its best,
nourish their audiences
in ways that make the dancing generated
a delightful, even ecstatic, flourishing for all engaged.

What attitudes and behaviors, then,
is the Spirit of the Creator's Christ
provoking among those with whom you are missioning
that might free you all for encounters with the Divine Delight?

Co-Creating God's Flourishing Future

Jazz at its best, like church at its best,
frees us to generate continuous improvement
in the contributions we make
to the liberation of all humanity
in the service of the creation's flourishing
intended by our Family of Creator.

What attitudes and behaviors, then,
is the Spirit of the Creator's Christ
provoking among those with whom you are missioning
that might draw you further into the swing of sanctifying significance
in contributing to the replenishing of God's goodness
throughout all creation?

Appendix

Laura Zerebeski (https://laurazee.com) is the Vancouver-based artist who painted "The Spirit of Jazz" / "The Trinity Trio" for Brentwood as our logo for our missioning with the jazz community. The painting is on the cover of this book and the line drawing that got it started is below. This is her interpretation of the work.

The Spirit of Jazz/The Trinity Trio started as a simple line drawing to illustrate Brian's reformulation of the Trinity in jazz.

Where God, the Creator, lays down the bass line.
Where Jesus Christ, the Redeemer, calls the melodies.
Where the Holy Spirit, the Energizer, jams with the harmonies of joy.

Visual representations of jazz typically focus on the musicians and the instruments. David Liebman, prominent jazz saxophonist, noted: "The nature of music is an abstraction—something you can't touch, you can't see. There is something about the non-tangible aspect that raises it to the realm of imagination, creativity and spirituality. But the spirit is also an abstraction because it, too, is something you can neither see nor touch."

How does one portray both jazz music and spirituality visually? Jazz is music that expresses the range of human emotion played by players who are collaborative and improvisational. It is also inherently joyful and accepting because the idea behind a good jam or improv session is to always say yes without judgment and build on each other's musical suggestions. One could also say that is a facet of spirituality.

The expressionists used colour and rapid brush strokes to depict emotion. I wanted to show a dynamic force that has expressive and generous qualities, so I used colour. All the colours! Rainbows symbolize inclusiveness, variety, beauty, and even reward via the myth of the pot of gold at end of rainbow. The expressionists would set colors against their opposites because red is always redder against green and blue bluer against orange. Like a good jam session, each colour has to combine with the others without losing itself and thereby make for a more vital whole. The swirls mimic and exaggerate the effect of light through smoke as one might see with stained glass and incense or even neon signage and cigarette smoke.

The three figures are somewhat incorporeal, though the hands and musical instruments have more weight and visual specificity than the heads. This fits because the heads represent thought while hands are action and instruments are the tools. Creative energy exists in the interplay between intention, action, and method.

Whenever I think about energy, I am reminded of an old physics joke, which fits in this context:

You matter.

Until you multiply yourself by the speed of light squared.

THEN YOU ENERGY.

Which is kind of like saying we're all potential energy waiting for an intangible factor to transform us into something even more significant. That's the essence of spirituality and perhaps we can sense that intangible means of transformation in jazz.

Bibliography

Alexander, Monty. *Impressions in Blue*. Cleveland: Telarc Jazz, 2003.

Barrett, Frank J., and Fry, Ronald E. *Appreciative Inquiry: A Positive Approach to Building Cooperative Capacity*. Chagrin Falls: Taos Institute, 2010.

Barrett, Frank J. *Yes to the Mess: Surprising Leadership Lessons from Jazz*. Boston: Harvard Business School Press, 2012.

Barris, Alex. *Oscar Peterson: A Musical Biography*. Toronto: HarperCollins, 2002.

Barth, Karl, *Prayer*. 50th Anniversary ed. Louisville: Westminster John Knox, 2002.

Bateson, Mary Catherine. *Composing a Life*. New York:Grove, 1989.

Beaumont, Susan. *How to Lead When You Don't Know Where You're Going: Leading in a Liminal Season*. Lanham: Rowman & Littlefield, 2019.

Bedford, Nancy Elizabeth. *Galatians*. Belief: A Theological Commentary on the Bible. Louisville: 2016.

Begbie, Jeremy S. *Resounding Truth: Christian Wisdom in the World of Music*. Grand Rapids: Baker Academic, 2007.

———. *Theology, Music and Time*. Cambridge Studies in Christian Doctrine. Cambridge: Cambridge University Press, 2000.

Benmergui, Ralph. *I Though He Was Dead: A Spiritual Memoir*. Hamilton: James Street North, 2021.

Berliner, Paul F. *Thinking in Jazz: The Infinite Art of Improvisation*. Chicago: University of Chicago Press, 1994.

Bivins, Jason C. *Spirits Rejoice: Jazz and American Religion*. Toronto: Oxford University Press, 2015.

Boschman, Nelson. "Then Sings my Soul: Towards a Theology of Jazz in Christian Worship." Regent College paper, Nov 14, 2001.

Boyatzis, Richard, and McKee, Annie. *Resonant Leadership: Renewing Yourself and Connecting with Others Through Mindfulness, Hope, and Compassion*. Boston: Harvard Business School Press, 2005.

Branson, Mark Lau. *Memories, Hopes, and Conversations: Appreciative Inquiry, Missional Engagement, and Congregational Change*. Lanham: Rowman & Littlefield, 2016.

Broadhead, Bradley K., *Jazz and Christian Freedom: Improvising Against the Grain of the West*. Eugene: Pickwick, 2018.

Brueggemann, Walter. *Sabbath as Resistance: Saying No to the Culture of Now*. Louisville: Westminster John Knox, 2014.

Buechner, Frederick. *Then and Now: A Memoir of Vocation*. New York: HarperOne, 1991.

Canadian Songwriters Hall of Fame. "Hymn to Freedom." https://www.cshf.ca/song/hymn-to-freedom.

Carter, William G. *Thriving on a Riff: Jazz and the Spiritual Life*. Minneapolis: Broadleaf, 2024.

Cho, Adrian. *The Jazz Process: Collaboration, Innovation, and Agility*. Toronto: Addison-Wesley, 2010.

Cressey, Paul Goalby. *The Taxi-Dance Hall: A Sociological Study in Commercialized Recreation and City Life*. Chicago: University of Chicago Press, 1932.

Davis, Miles, with Troupe, Quincy. *Miles: The Autobio*graphy. New York: Touchstone, 1989.

Des Cotes, Rob. *Jazz Is . . .: A Philosophy of Jazz in the Groove of Life*. North Vancouver: Omega, 2001.

Drummond, Fred. *All That Jazz: Learning to hear the kingdom tune in a new setting*. London: Authentic, 2007.

Edgar, William. *A Supreme Love: The Music of Jazz and the Hope of the Gospel*. Downers Grove: IVP Academic, 2022.

Fensham, Charles. *Emerging from the Dark Age Ahead: The Future of the North American Church*. Ottawa: Novalis, 2008.

———. *To the Nations of the Earth: A Missional Spirituality*. Toronto: Clements Academic, 2013.

Fraser, Brian, *Generating a Great Governance Groove*. Vancouver: Kindle, 2017.

———. *Jazzthink: Playing with the Stuff of Success*. Victoria: Trafford, 2004.

Freire, Paulo. *Pedagogy of Freedom: Ethics, Democracy, and Civic Courage*. Lanhan: Rowman & Littlefield, 1998.

Friedman, Edwin H. *A Failure of Nerve: Leadership in the Age of the Quick Fix*. New York: Seabury, 2007.

Fujimura, Makoto. *Art + Faith: A Theology of Making*. New Haven: Yale University Press, 2020.

Gelinas, Robert. *Finding the Groove: Composing a Jazz-Shaped Faith*. Grand Rapids: Zondervan, 2009.

Glanville, Mark. *Improvising Church: Scripture as the Source of Harmony, Rhythm, and Soul*. Downers Grove: IVP Academic, 2024.

Gottlieb, Robert, ed. *Reading Jazz*. New York: Vintage, 1996.

Hayman, Brian. *A Tale of Two Keyboards*. Oakville: Getting in the Groove, 2018

———. *Conversations on the Edge: Jazz and the Art of Reimagining*. Oakville: Getting in the Groove, nd.

Heclo, Hugh. *On Thinking Institutionally*. Boston: Paradigm, 2008.

Heltzel, Peter Goodwin, *Resurrection City: A Theology of Improvisation*. Grand Rapids: Eerdmans, 2012.

Hall, Douglas John. *What Christianity is Not: An Exercise in Negative Theology*. Eugene: Cascade, 2013.

Heschel, Abraham Joshua. *Who Is Man?* Stanford: Standford University Press, 1965.

hooks, bell. *Teaching Community: A Pedagogy of Hope*. New York: Routledge, 2003.

Horne, Gerald. *Jazz and Justice: Racism and the Political Economy of the Music*. New York: Monthly Review,2019.

Jennings, Willie James. "Seeing God in Jazz." *Divinity* 11 (2011) 23–25.

———. *Acts*. Belief: A Theological Commentary on the Bible. Louisville: Westminster John Knox, 2017.

Jones, Kirby Byro., *The Jazz of Preaching: How to Preach with Great Freedom and Joy*. Nashville: Abingdon, 2004.

Jones, L. Gregory and Hogue, Andrew P. *Navigating the Future: Traditioned Innovation for Wilder Seas*. Nashville: Abingdon, 2021.

Joseph, Chief Robert. *Namwayut-We Are All One: A Pathway to Reconciliation*. Vancouver: Page Two, 2022.

Kamoche, Ken, Cunha, Migel Pina e, and Cunha, Joao Viera da, eds. *Organizational Improvisation*. New York: Routledge, 2002.

Kao, John. *Jamming: The Art and Discipline of Business Creativity*. New York: HarperCollins, 1996.

Kim, Grace Ji-Sun. *Reimagining Spirit: Wind, Breath, and Vibration*. Eugene: Cascade, 2020.

King, Martin Luther Jr. "Jazz." https://jazzbuffalo.org/2019/01/21/the-essay-by-martin-luther-king-jr-that-lives-large-in-jazz.

Koransky, Jason. "Editorial." *DownBeat* 25 (July 2001) 8.

Lansdowne, Carmen. *Wearing a Broken Indigene Heart on the Sleeve of Christian Mission*. Winnipeg: CMU Press, 2025.

Lee, Boyung. *Transforming Congregations through Community: Faith Formation from the Seminary to the Church*. Louisville: Westminster John Knox, 2013.

Lees, Gene. *Oscar Peterson: The Will to Swing*. Toronto: Prospero, 2008.

Lochhead, David. *The Dialogical Imperative: A Christian Reflection on Interfaith Dialogue*. Maryknoll: Orbis, 1989.

Marsalis, Wynton. *Moving to Higher Ground: How Jazz Can Change Your Life*. New York: Random House, 2008.

Moltmann, Jurgen. *Experiences of God*. London: SCM Press, 2012.

———. *The Spirit of Life: A Universal Affirmation*. Minneapolis: Fortress, 1992.

———. *Theology of Play*. New York: Harper & Row, 1972.

Morrison, Bradley T. "Already-mission: Expanding Congregational Mission." *Missiology: An International Review* 42 (2014) 271–283.

Moss III, Otis, *Dancing in the Darkness: Spiritual Lessons for Thriving in Turbulent Times*. New York: Simon & Schuster, 2022.

Myers, Chad, and Enns, Elaine. *Ambassadors of Reconciliation, Volume I.* New Testament Reflections on Restorative Justice and Peacemaking. Maryknoll: Orbis, 2009.

Nachmanovich, Stephen. *Free Play: The Power of Improvisation in Life and the Arts.* New York. Jeremy P. Tarcher/Putnam, 1990.

———. *The Art of Is: Improvising as a Way of Life.* Novato: New World Library, 2019.

Pederson, Ann. *God, Creation, and All That Jazz: A Process of Composition and Improvisation.* Nashville: Chalise, 2000.

Peters, Gary. *The Philosophy of Improvisation.* Chicago: University of Chicago Press, 2009.

Picard, Michael, ed. *Café Conversations: Participatory Philosophy in Public Spaces.* Rock's Mills: Rock's Mills, 2025.

Porter, Mark. *Ecologies of Resonance in Christian Musicking.* New York: Oxford University Press, 2020.

Reynolds, Thomas E. "JAZZ: Human Transformation in a Musical Key." *Touchstone* 27 (2009) 32–38.

Rigby, Cynthia L. *Holding Faith: A Practical Introduction to Christian Doctrine.* Nashville: Abingdon, 2018.

Roxburgh, Alan J. *Joining God in the Great Unraveling: Where We Are & What I've Learned.* Eugene: Cascade, 2021.

Roxburgh, Alan, and Branson, Mark Lau. *Leadership, God's Agency, & Disruptions: Confronting Modernity's Wager.* Eugene: Cascade, 2020.

Roxburgh, Alan, and Searle, Roy. *Forming Communities of Hope in the Great Unraveling.* Eugene: Cascade, 2025.

Schein, Edgar H. and Schein, Peter A. *Humble Inquiry: The Gentle Art of Asking Instead of Telling.* 3rd ed. San Francisco: Berrett-Koehler, 2025.

Small, Christopher. *Musicking: The Meanings of Performing and Listening.* Hanover: Wesleyan University Press, 1998.

Smith, C. Christopher. *How the Body of Christ Talks: Recovering the Practice of Conversation in the Church.* Grand Rapids: Brazos, 2019.

———. *The Virtue of Dialogue: Becoming a Thriving Church Through Conversation.* Indianapolis: Englewood, 2025

Steed, Janna Tull. *Duke Ellinton: A Spiritual Biography.* New York: Crossroad, 1999.

Thurman, Howard. *Meditations of the Heart.* Boston: Beacon, 1994.

Thompson, Curt. *The Soul of Shame: Retelling the Stories We Believe About Ourselves.* Downers Grove: IVP, 2015.

Tobin, Penelope. *The Jazz of Business: Leadership in a New Groove.* London: Dodgem, 2012.

Tuttle, Shea. *Exactly As You Are: The Life and Faith of Mister Rogers.* Grand Rapids: Eerdmans, 2019.

Wells, Samuel. *Improvisation: The Drama of Christian Ethics.* Grand Rapids, Brazos, 2004.

West, Cornell. *Brother West: Living and Loving Out Loud: A Memoir*. New York: Smiley, 2010.

———. *The Cornel West Reader*. New York: Basic Civitas, 1999.

Williamson, Maryanne, *Return to Love: Reflections on the Principles of A Course in Miracles*. New York: HarperOne, 1996.

Woodley, Randy S. *Indigenous Theology and the Western Worldview: A Decolonized Approach to Christian Doctrine*. Grand Rapids:Baker Academic, 2022.

Zohar, Danah. *Rewiring the Corporate Brain: Using the New Science to Rethink How We Structure and Lead Organizations*. San Francisco: Berrett-Koehler, 1997.

www.ingramcontent.com/pod-product-compliance
Lightning Source LLC
LaVergne TN
LVHW050613100826
845148LV00011B/1566

* 9 7 9 8 3 8 5 2 7 0 0 2 6 *